Reducing Inter-generational Ethnic Poverty

This book looks at human capital development and provides an explanation for why cognitive development varies among ethnic groups. The book uses an interdisciplinary approach to examine inter-generational ethnic poverty. It puts forth an argument that the ethnic poverty gap can be reduced, and to do so we need a broader view of human capital which considers the match between the nature of the economy and the specific capabilities needed. The book focuses on the interrelationship between developmental psychology and socio-economic status and argues that the most important relationship in a knowledge economy is actually the one between a parent and a child.

The book begins by looking at cultures and assimilation and investigates the link between education, culture and socio-economic status. It also attempts to answer the question of what the link between culture, parents and children's ability is and why ethnic groups vary in their nurturing. It delves into how parenting and cognitive development are interrelated.

This thought-provoking book concludes with an emphasis on nurture and how it may alleviate ethnic poverty and shape social policies. The book provides a strong thesis to counter explanations based on racial and genetic superiority.

Greg Clydesdale lectures at Lincoln University, New Zealand. His expertise centres on economic growth and welfare on which he has authored four books. He has conducted staff training and consultancy programmes for public and private organizations including the Ngai Tahu Development Corporation (a Maori tribe).

Reducing Inter-generational Ethnic Poverty

Economics, Psychology and Culture

Greg Clydesdale

Routledge
Taylor & Francis Group
LONDON AND NEW YORK

First published 2021
by Routledge
2 Park Square, Milton Park, Abingdon, Oxon OX14 4RN

and by Routledge
52 Vanderbilt Avenue, New York, NY 10017

Routledge is an imprint of the Taylor & Francis Group, an informa business

British Library Cataloguing in Publication Data
A catalogue record for this book is available from the British Library

Library of Congress Cataloging-in-Publication Data
A catalog record has been requested for this book

ISBN: 978-0-367-61629-8 (hbk)
ISBN: 978-1-003-10577-0 (ebk)

Typeset in Galliard
by Taylor & Francis Books

Contents

Illustrations

Figures

Tables

1 Introduction

In 2007, Nobel Prize-winner James Watson issued his forecast for Africa saying he was 'inherently gloomy' about the prospects for the continent. However, it wasn't his forecast that upset people but his explanation why he expected poor outcomes. He said 'all our social policies are based on the fact that their intelligence is the same as ours—where all the testing says not really'.[1]

Watson was not the first to make these claims. They have been made repeatedly ever since intelligence tests found differences between ethnic groups. In 1994, Herrnstein and Murray's book *The Bell Curve* claimed that socio-economic outcomes were a consequence of intelligence differences between ethnic groups.[2] This prompted the American Psychological Association to issue a response in which they questioned many of the claims in the book.[3] Nevertheless, they acknowledged a difference in IQ scores between ethnic groups. They also acknowledged there is not an adequate explanation for those differences.

A number of explanations have been offered for the differences. These include the fact that IQ tests measure styles of intelligence that favour white people. Another explanation questions the very notions of intelligence and races. However, the most common explanations focus on the environment. Ethnic groups vary in their achievement because they live in different environments and these generate different developmental outcomes. In particular, minority ethnic groups experience lower socio-economic status, health and nutrition. They also experience structural disadvantages including discrimination and cultural trauma.

However, there is disagreement whether these explanations account for all the gap in intelligence scores. A number of writers, such as Eric Turkheimer, argue that environmental forces are a factor, but they do not account for all the gap in intelligence.[4] Nicholas Mackintosh wonders if it is indeed possible to know what extent the environment explains the gap.[5]

It is hard to definitively state whether enough evidence exists as, despite their skills in scientific method, academics are still prone to bias reflecting their training and socio-political views. For example, James Watson is a geneticist, so he favoured a genetic explanation. Nevertheless, the debate will remain until the gap is firmly closed. This book hopes to close that gap, or at least make it a little smaller, but what is needed to do that? James Watson made it clear what would close the gap for him. He stated that he would like to see new knowledge that shows

> nurture is much more important than nature but I haven't seen any knowledge and there's a difference on the average between blacks and whites on IQ tests. I would say the difference is genetic.[6]

In other words, to close the gap we need to pay closer attention to the nurturing process in different cultures. The father of economics, Adam Smith, lived in an ethnically homogeneous society, but he made an explicit judgement that differences in outcomes were caused by nurture not nature. He claimed:

> The difference between the most dissimilar characters, between a philosopher and a common street porter, for example, seems to arise not so much from nature, as from habit, custom and education.[7]

Adam Smith believed we are born as relative equals but about the age of 6–8,

> they come to be employed in very different occupations. The difference in talents comes to be taken notice of, and widens by degrees, till at last the vanity of the philosopher is willing to acknowledge scarce any resemblance.[8]

But this leaves us with unanswered questions. What are the 'habits and customs and educational differences' that create these differences in outcomes, and why do ethnic groups vary in their nurturing? We also need to know why these differences affect cognitive/intellectual outcomes.

The problem to date is many social scientists have deliberately shut the door on some nurture explanations. In particular, they will not consider a link between culture and poverty. As Princeton Professor Douglas Massey notes:

> For decades, it was not possible to use culture and poverty in the same sentence in polite sociological company.[9]

That means they have closed the door on a corridor that could lead to solutions. Fortunately, not all scientists have ignored this direction. Anthropologists, developmental, educational and cross-cultural psychologists have all produced research that can help us understand the problem. This book draws on their work.

However, it must be stressed that this book is not about intelligence but economic performance. The book hopes that by gaining a greater understanding of cultural and economic differences, we can reduce poverty among disadvantaged ethnic groups. The focus is on wealth and poverty to which the issue of intelligence contributes. To close the poverty gap, we must open the door on a direction that many social scientists have not wanted to take. We need to understand the link between human capabilities, culture and the economy. In particular, three questions need to be answered:

- What is the link between culture and economic systems?
- What is the link between culture, parenting and children's ability?
- What are the implications for policy?

Wealth creation and wealth distribution

One of the most enduring socio-economic problems facing academics and policy-makers is the experience of ethnic groups with a high propensity for poverty. By definition, it means that members of society do not equally experience that society's benefits. At its worst, it contributes to a social structure where class divisions are characterised by ethnicity.[10]

This book examines the tendency of some ethnic groups to experience intergenerational poverty. Each ethnic group has its own particular history and characteristics, so a policy repertoire is needed that can accommodate those differences. Hence, the aim of this book is to provide an alternative explanation for this phenomenon and contribute to the policy options available.

Many explanations for poverty concentrate on power relations and structural forces, and with good reason. There is no end of examples where those at the top have used their position to take a disproportionate share of their society's resources. This can be seen in feudal society in which serfs laboured in the fields to produce output that was appropriated by land-owning gentry. More recently, we need only think of the slave labour that African Americans were forced to endure.

In theory, a market economy is less likely to create such disparities as wage rates are determined by a person's skills and the demand for those skills. However, market distortions can occur if a group gain a position in the market with significant negotiating power. For example, many CEOs in modern corporations have acquired positions whereby their incomes far exceed their economic contribution.

Structural explanations of poverty are related to power-based explanations. These do not necessarily state that a group is exploiting its power, but the structure of society is one which benefits their group at the expense of others. Once again, the academic research to support this view is boundless. Hence, there is good reason to view poverty and income distribution in terms of power relations and structural deficiencies. However, these explanations have not led to successful policies, perhaps because discrimination still exists.

A problem comes when these views shut out other explanations that contribute to the problem, in particular if we do not consider how wealth and income is created, in which case poverty is reduced to income distribution. Poverty is seen as a zero-sum game where one ethnic group benefits at another's expense.

It is easy to believe that the existing level of wealth in society is the natural level, and poverty can be solved by simply distributing it more equitably. However, this view provides a false view of poverty and prosperity. In particular, it ignores the process of wealth creation by which poverty is eradicated.

For most of humanity, the natural level of wealth has been one significantly lower than that which exists today. Modern humans appeared about 200,000 years ago and, for most of the time since then, lived in nomadic tribal groups, hunting and gathering whatever their environment provided. By today's standards, the natural level of wealth was one of poverty. Leaps in welfare occurred between 10,000 and 20,000 years ago with the domestication of animals, and the advent of agriculture about 12,000 years ago. Another leap in wealth occurred in those societies that experienced 'civilisation' and the birth of early market economies which enabled people to trade. Finally, 200 years ago, an industrial revolution occurred which propelled human standards to even greater heights.

The prosperity we enjoy today is the result of these wealth creating advances; however, not all ethnic groups experienced these leaps. Some remained in subsistence agriculture, others were hunters and gathers. Consequently, ethnic groups varied in the level of wealth they produced. To exploit these changes, societies needed to adopt new skills, values and knowledge. It required a cultural shift. However, many ethnic groups have not adopted the cultural components that exist in today's knowledge economies.

The idea that cultural characteristics can determine income is highly controversial, given its potential misuse by racial supremacists and, predictably, researchers have been hesitant to enter this arena. Policy-makers and researchers have tended towards the safe. However, if we are too cautious, we may miss opportunities to help improve the welfare of the people that we are trying to protect. If academics and policy-makers are to create effective solutions, we must keep our eye on the goal – that is, to improve the material welfare of these groups.

Material poverty is the absence of material wealth, and there are big variations in the wealth produced. Different ethnic groups may populate the same territory but achieve different levels of economic prosperity. For example, Europeans settled in North America and Australasia, and achieved a much higher level of material prosperity than those living there before them. The pre-existing poverty could not have been a result of discrimination nor colonisation as the Europeans had not yet arrived.

Of course, this assumes that these ethnic groups desired material wealth. They may have been happy in their relative material poverty given the welfare gains from other aspects of their lives. This raises a possible criticism of this book in that its focus is on material wealth. Hence, it is important to make an important clarification. That is, although this book aims to reduce material poverty (for those who desire it), this book does not assume that material prosperity is the only form of welfare.

Nevertheless, material poverty is generally seen as an undesirable state and history reveals that ethnic groups vary in their ability to produce wealth. In 2010, Putterman and Weil constructed a matrix that linked a country's economic development to the history of the population's ancestors including their experience with agriculture.[11] They found that the ancestors of the existing population had an important determinant on income levels. This research has been supported by Easterly and Levine (2012) who revealed that a large population of European ancestry provides advantages for economic development.[12]

These findings are supported by recent research on genetic distance; that is the length of time that has passed since two populations shared a common ancestor.[13]

The research strongly suggests that economic development is affected by ethnic traits that have been transmitted across generations over the very long run. However, a problem comes in determining which traits are important, in particular are they biological traits or cultural? If biological, it returns us to the genetic/racial arguments raised at the beginning of the book.

The alternative is culture; however, cultural traits such as values and norms are much harder to measure from a long-term macroeconomic perspective. With this in mind, it is important to differentiate between culture, ethnicity and race. There are many definitions of race which commonly refer to people of common ancestry. Some definitions include a cultural aspect, but most focus on physical characteristics, that is those characteristics determined by biology/genetic forces. Defining race in terms of biology allows us to differentiate it from ethnicity which 'is viewed as representing shared practices, beliefs and values linked to 'nationality, common ancestry, and/or immigration experiences'.[14]

Lastly, culture is a man-made phenomenon that 'represents ways of living that have been developed by a group of people to meet their biological, psychological and emotional needs. Transmitted inter-generationally, culture encompasses social norms, roles, beliefs, values and practices and serves to provide guidelines for the socialization of children and successful adult functioning.'[15]

There are many definitions of culture, but one of interest is that by anthropologist Roy Rappaport who describes culture as a 'tool' with which society adapts to nature. He states, culture is:

> A part of a distinctive means by which a local population maintains itself in an ecosystem and by which a regional population maintains and coordinates its groups and distributes them over the land.[16]

This 'tool' includes knowledge, skills and organisations that are created in response to their environment. This raises a number of questions. In particular, how does culture change as the environment and resource base change? For example, was a change in culture required when humans changed from a hunting and gathering society to one based on agriculture? Clearly, to benefit from the new economy, people would need to acquire new skills and knowledge. Would this change education and parenting practices?

Another consideration in reading this book is the variation that occurs within populations. If researchers reveal that, on average, one ethnic group performs better than another, it does not mean that all members of that group succeed or fail. The researchers are merely presenting an average. When an economy evolves, its members will advance at different rates. That, of course, means that the solutions in this book may also benefit poorer members of the more successful ethnic groups.

This book focuses on ethnicity and culture, with a particular focus on parenting behaviours and economic welfare. Being non-biological, this approach offers an exciting possibility to solve some forms of poverty. If we can identify which characteristics are passed on inter-generationally, it may be possible to craft a solution by targeting those characteristics. By contrast, it is more difficult to develop policies that target racial or biological characteristics.

The fact that some cultures are better at producing wealth can lead the wealthier cultures to take a condescending view of the poorer ones. Hence, the next chapter examines how the idea of cultural superiority and enforced assimilation led to a backlash against studying a link between culture and poverty among many social scientists. Ironically, at the same time, economists were noting that differences between cultures have a significant influence on wealth creation. Explanations for some groups experiencing poverty are examined.

The third chapter examines the question 'what is the link between culture and economic systems?' It reveals that the economy and resource base have a huge influence on people's values, motivations and beliefs. It also determines the capabilities needed to prosper with those resources. It is also noted that a cultural shift occurred in Europe in the late eighteenth century which facilitated greater prosperity. The Enlightenment and scientific revolution heralded a greater use of knowledge for wealth and welfare. Western nations took the lead in developing a knowledge-based economy. As a consequence, Westerners excelled in wealth creation and by contrast, other cultures remained in relative poverty.

Chapter 4 examines the question 'What is the link between parenting, culture and children's ability?' It is noted that a society's resource base strongly influences the behaviours, capabilities and values passed on by parents. Of note is the tendency of tribal societies to focus on the development of their children's motors skills, in contrast to the modern emphasis on cognitive skills. This suggests a reason why cognitive skills are low in some cultures is parental nurturing focuses on motor skills, not on cognitive skills. The focus on cognitive skills has only been necessary since the development of a knowledge economy.

The fifth chapter notes that education plays an important role in determining future earnings, and it is significant that many poorer ethnic groups also perform badly at school. There is a strong body of evidence that shows poverty reduces the potential for parents to guide and support their children's education. Hence, their academic outcomes suffer. However, Chinese students seem to excel where other minorities fail. This leads to an examination of Chinese parenting practice. The Chinese should be blocked by the same barriers that block other ethnic minorities, but the Chinese make these barriers look insignificant. This places the spotlight back on cultural differences. We then consider the practices that developmental psychologists have been recommending for contemporary parenting and the best development outcomes for children.

Chapter 6 examines neuroplasticity in more detail, and the importance of parents and the home for neural development. This is followed by an examination of how cultures have different views on a child's development, that is, ethnotheories.

The seventh chapter returns to the economic literature and notes that since the 1960s human capital has been recognised as an important driver of economic growth that creates wealth and reduces poverty. It draws on evolutionary economics which focuses on the acquisition and persistence of behavioural routines.

Acquired behaviours can be slow to change including parental practice. This can create a wealth gap if behaviours are maintained by people moving to a new economic system.

Because ethnicity and low socio-economic status are so closely entwined, it is hard to distinguish if poor parental practices are a consequence of poverty or ethnicity. This is discussed in Chapter 8. Traditional explanations have favoured poverty as the principal cause but they have not sufficiently disentangled the two factors. This difficulty in pin-pointing causation creates problems in developing effective policy. Recent research has suggested this impasse could be overcome, not by focusing on poverty or ethnicity but by focusing on parental practice. This addresses the problem more directly.

On this basis, Chapter 9 argues that parental programmes could enhance a number of areas of development that impact on a child's future welfare. These include cognitive stimulation, language and vocabulary, self-control and social skills, and the provision of structure. In confirming the importance of children's home experiences for their early academic development, studies like these offer exciting hope that interventions can be created that reduce gaps in wealth and academic output by fostering awareness in parents of what they can do to facilitate their children's development.

This is followed by case studies of two ethnic groups with different historical experiences, that is Maori and Pacific emigrants to New Zealand. One group was colonised while the other emigrated to their new land, yet they have attained similar educational and material outcomes. Living in the Pacific area, both Maori and Pacific people were historically cut off from global knowledge flows. Hence their cultures never acquired important capabilities for a knowledge economy. To hasten integration into the modern economy, government policies were based on policies that effect income redistribution and maintain cultural heritage. However, they have failed to achieve their goals.

The fight against poverty is based on the idea that increased material resources can improve human welfare, but is this true? Could it be that materialistic Westerners are imposing their views on other cultures? These questions are considered in Chapter 11.

Many academics have called for policy to focus on parents and culture, but there has been much resistance to doing so. The last chapter discusses some of the reasons why this may be so, including a fear of blaming the victim, cultural inertia, stakeholders and current academic paradigms. However, culture is a prime influence on parental practice, which in turn influences the behaviours and capabilities that generate wealth.

There is a need for new policy tools to overcome poverty. This can be done in a manner that respects autonomy and freedom of choice. The days of enforced assimilation are long gone, but we can help those parents who want their children to succeed.

This book takes an interdisciplinary approach to this problem. In particular, it draws on the research of educational and developmental psychologists who have observed important differences in the development practices and outcomes of ethnic groups. Their research has important implications for human capital development and the resulting wealth levels.

Parenting lays the foundation for human capital development, and the practices that occur at the earliest stage of life need to be placed at the fore-front of economic thinking. This does not mean that ethnic groups are failing because of poor or incompetent parenting. On the contrary, this book reveals that African parents can actually be 'superior' to Europeans in developing their children's motor skills. With this in mind, researchers need to stop using words like 'superior' and 'inferior' and start thinking in terms of being fit for purpose. That is to say, what parental methods are best for a knowledge economy?

This book does not attempt to explain poverty for all ethnic groups, nor is its intention to challenge or criticise current explanations. Many ethnic groups have suffered from policies and structures that are racist or discriminatory in nature. However, it is important to acknowledge that there are many causes of poverty and what may be a cause for one ethnic group may not a cause for another. Also, poverty is often not a case of one cause but a case of a number of factors working in combination. All influences need to be addressed if we are to reduce poverty.

Many social scientists dislike the views of economists who focus on human capital, but human capital explanations are not the antithesis of structural explanations. Economists know that human capital does not explain all variance in income, and many forces are at work. Nevertheless, human capital is an important factor which cannot be ignored.

This book focuses on poverty among marginalised ethnic groups. Although it was not the intention of this book to enter the debate on racial comparisons of intelligence, in examining human capital development this book does have relevance to that debate. Tests have shown inter-racial differences in intelligence. Racial and genetic explanations exist for these differences because the role of nurturing has not been adequately explained. This book describes differences in nurturing and why those differences exist. If children have experienced nurturing that favours cognitive skills, they will do better on intelligence tests devised in the West as these focus on cognitive processing.

The first five years of a child's life are vitally important for neural development in the brain. Neural pathways are being shaped and strengthened by the child's interaction with the wider world. Hence, the home environment and parental practice play a vital role in a child's development. When our knowledge of neural development and parenting is combined with our knowledge on culture, we have an explanation for intelligence differences that is not racial or genetic.

Hence, this book argues that the view advocated by James Wilkins is wrong. Genes only provide the template for development. It is the environment in the first years of a child's life that provides the expression of those genes. It is nurture not nature. Until now, we have not had an explanation why nurturing would vary. This book provides that explanation and hopefully has enough explanatory power to end thoughts of racial and genetic superiority.

Notes

1 Tidey Alice & Associated Press (2019). Nobel Prize Winning scientist stripped of last honorary titles over racist comments. *Euronews*, 13 January. Downloaded 15 January from https://www.euronews.com/2019/01/13/nobel-prize-winning-scientist-stripped-of-last-honorary-titles-over-racist-comments.
2 Herrnstein, R.J., & Murray, C. (1994). *The Bell Curve: Intelligence and Class Structure in American Life*. New York: Free Press.
3 Neisser, U., Boodoo, G., Bouchard Jr, T.J., Boykin, A.W., Brody, N., Ceci, S.J., …, & Urbina, S. (1996). Intelligence: Knowns and unknowns. *American Psychologist, 51*(2), 77.
4 Turkheimer, E. (2011). Genetics and human agency: Comment on Dar-Nimrod and Heine. *Psychological Bulletin*, 137 (5), 825–828.
5 Mackintosh, N.J. (2011). *IQ and Human Intelligence*, 2nd edition. Oxford: Oxford University Press.
6 American Masters (2018). *Decoding Watson*, American Masters and WNET.
7 Smith Adam (1976). *An Inquiry into the Nature and Causes of the Wealth of Nations* (Ed. R.H. Campbell & A.S. Skinner). Indianapolis: Liberty Press, I ii.4.
8 Ibid.
9 Massey, D.S., McCall, L., Tomaskovic-Devey, D., Avent-Holt, D., Monin, P., Forgues, B., & Wang, T. (2014). Understanding inequality through the lens of cultural processes: On Lamont, Beljean and Clair 'What is Missing? Cultural Processes and Causal Pathways to Inequality'. *Socio-Economic Review, 12*, 610–614.
10 Faist, T. (1994). States, markets, and immigrant minorities: Second-generation Turks in Germany and Mexican–Americans in the United States in the 1980s. *Comparative Politics*, 439–460. Macpherson, C. (1977). Polynesians in New Zealand: An Emerging Eth-Class? In D. Pitt (Ed.), *Social Class in New Zealand*. Auckland: Longman Paul, pp. 99–112.
11 Putterman, L., & Weil, D.N. (2010). Post-1500 population flows and the long-run determinants of economic growth and inequality. *The Quarterly Journal of Economics, 125*(4), 1627–1682.
12 Easterly, W., & Levine, R. (2012). The European Origins of Comparative Development. *NBER Working Paper, 18162.*
13 Spolaore, E., & Wacziarg, R. (2013). How deep are the roots of economic development? *Journal of Economic Literature, 51*(2), 325–369. Spolaore, E., & Wacziarg, R. (2009). The diffusion of development. *The Quarterly Journal of Economics, 124*(2), 469–529.
14 Hill, N.E., McBride, M.V., & Anderson, V.D. (2005). Sociocultural contexts of African American families. In V.C. McLoyd, N.E. Hill, K.A. Dodge, K.A. Dodge, & M. Putallaz (Eds.), *African American Family Life: Ecological and Cultural Diversity*, vol. 2. New York: Guilford Press, p. 23
15 Le, H.N., Ceballo, R., Chao, R., Hill, N.E., Murry, V.M., & Pinderhughes, E.E. (2008). Excavating culture: Disentangling ethnic differences from contextual influences in parenting. *Applied Development Science, 12*(4), 163–175.
16 Rappaport, R.A. (1968). *Pigs for the Ancestors*. New Haven: Yale University Press, p. 233.

2 Assimilation, cultural superiority and poverty

There has been a great reluctance among social scientists to consider a link between culture and poverty. This reluctance emerged in the shadow of Oscar Lewis's 1959 book *Five Families.* Lewis studied the daily life of five Mexican families. He spent a day with each family and analysed their behaviour under the headings of material culture, economic life, social relations, religious life, interpersonal relations and so on. At the end of his study he concluded that poverty creates a subculture of its own; a culture of poverty that cuts across regional, rural-urban and national boundaries.[1]

According to Lewis, poor people adapted a value system in response to their marginal position in society. This value system was adopted to 'cope with feelings of hopelessness and despair that develop' when the people realise 'the improbability of achieving success in terms of the values and goals of the larger society'.[2] The key traits of this value system were fatalism and low levels of aspiration.[3] Lewis says:

> The people in the culture of poverty have a strong feeling of marginality, of helplessness, of dependency, of not belonging. They are like aliens in their own country, convinced that the existing institutions do not serve their interests and needs. Along with this feeling of powerlessness is a widespread feeling of inferiority, of personal unworthiness.[4]

The problem is, once this culture comes into existence, it perpetuates itself from generation to generation. Children are exposed to these values and traits from their parents and have acquired them by the age of 6 or 7. Hence, when they become adults, they are 'not psychologically geared to take full advantage of the changing conditions or increased opportunities that may appear in their lifetime'.[5]

The poor accept that poverty is their fate and there is little use in trying hard for a better position in life. The effect is to create a poverty-perpetuating system. Hence Lewis argues that improving economic opportunities by themselves will not solve poverty. He does not deny the importance of improving opportunities. In fact, he says this is 'absolutely essential and of the highest priority', but more is needed to break this value system.

Lewis states that not everyone who lives in poverty develops a 'culture of poverty'. He listed four groups who avoided this outcome. First are primitive and preliterate societies. They are poor as a result of poor technology or natural resources, or both, but they have an integrated and self-sufficient culture which does not produce the traits identified by Lewis.

He also states that the Jews of eastern Europe avoided this culture as they have a tradition of literacy, place great value on learning and have strong community organisation. He also excluded the lower castes of India and, admitting his limited knowledge, speculates that socialist countries do not possess a culture of poverty.

It requires certain circumstances to occur for a culture of poverty to develop, Most frequently, this occurs when a stratified social and economic system is breaking down or is being replaced by another. This could be seen in the transition from feudalism to capitalism or during periods of rapid technological change. He also traced it to imperial conquest when native social and economic structures were smashed, or in times of detribalisation as seen in Africa.

Lewis backed up his work with studies of other groups. He had hoped that his work would enlighten and unify people in the fight against poverty; however, he did not get the response he expected. In fact, he was pilloried. His work was criticised for being inconsistent and contradictory.[6] There was doubt thrown on his belief that all members of a group share this culture, and there were questions over the link between values and perception, and attitudes and behaviour.[7] Most important, social scientists did not agree that poor were restricted by fatalism. By endowing the poor with a defeatist view, he was accused of blaming the victim for their impoverishment.[8]

Small, Harding and Lamont (2010) acknowledged the legitimacy of many of the criticisms but noted that many of the criticisms seemed to have a political basis.[9] This is because a culture of poverty supported a conservative agenda. An example of this is Carol Stack (1974) who states that the culture of poverty

> has a fundamental political nature. The ideas matter most to political and scientific groups attempting to rationalize why some Americans have failed to make it in American society ... They want to believe that raising the income of the poor would not change their life styles or values, but merely funnel greater sums of money into bottomless, self-destructing pits.[10]

As a consequence, left-leaning scholars were unwilling to consider cultural factors when explaining poverty and inequality.[11] This raises a serious concern that the welfare of marginalised groups is being sacrificed because academics and researchers with strong political views will not consider some explanations that might lead to solutions. Small, Harding and Lamont (2010) make a strong statement on this tendency saying:

> We hope we have made clear why we strongly disagree. None of the three editors of this volume happen to fall on the right of the political spectrum, but our political orientation is beside the point. Whether, when, and how cultural tools and cultural constrains matter is ultimately an empirical not a political question.[12]

An example of how this issue has been linked to political position can be seen in the complaint that Lewis was 'blaming the victim'. When Lewis said that cultures had certain traits that inclined them to poverty, he was accused of saying they were responsible for their state. However, if the blame lies with the rest of society, then society has an obligation to introduce policies and re-distribute money to remedy the situation.

Of course, blame is not necessary for a government to commit to solving poverty. The benefits of poverty reduction are too great to be described in detail in this chapter, but they include reduction in crime, benefit payments, increased taxation revenues as well as individual benefits such as improved health and welfare. In fact, an argument that relies on blame can be counter-productive and arouse defensive attitudes, resistance and polarisation.

Of course, there are many examples where ethnic groups have been disadvantaged by others. Two of the most obvious are slavery and segregation in the United States and apartheid in South Africa. But sometimes, misfortune may be no one's fault. It is a consequence of forces that no human engineered. For example, no one chooses the culture they are born into. Nor do they choose whether they are born into a tribal or knowledge economy. Cultural characteristics are often shaped by forces that occurred decades, maybe centuries, before the current generation.

There is one area where academics have been willing to accept a link between culture and poverty in marginalised ethnic groups. This is in the discussion of cultural trauma. This view argues that negative historical forces that impacted on a community have ongoing implications for their descendants. In particular, colonisation was a process in which they were overwhelmed by the technological, military and economic power of the coloniser.[13] They tried to resist this process but endured violence and excessive atrocities, the trauma from which continues to this day.

Under colonisation, the indigenous culture was denied autonomous development, and its members were expected to assimilate into the dominant culture. The colonisers believed the indigenous culture was backward when compared to their own. This backwardness was used as rationale for enforced change. Clearly, there are problems with this process, starting with the strong possibility of self-serving bias affecting the judgement of the colonisers.

The new culture might possess military, economic and technological supremacy, but there are other aspects by which a culture can be measured including social and spiritual aspects. Even if we were to take the position that the colonisers were culturally 'superior', it raises serious concerns whether this justifies change, particularly when change is forced on people who don't want it. It also reveals hypocrisy given that 'liberty' is one of the values that characterise many colonising cultures.

This colonisation has a negative effect on indigenous people psychologically and psycho-socially. Impacts on individuals included pervasive distrust, inaction, inertia, silence, indecision, fatalism and ambivalence.[14] These features then became characteristics of the culture that hold back its development.

The irony is that colonisation is one of the activities that Lewis recognised as creating a marginalised mindset, but few if any of the articles on cultural/colonial trauma cite him. Lewis stated:

> Often the culture of poverty results from imperial conquest in which the native social and economic structure is smashed and the natives are maintained in a servile colonial status, sometimes for many generations. It can also occur in the process of detribalisation, such as that now going on in Africa.[15]

When considering cultural trauma, it is accepted that Native Americans have experienced terrible injustices. In what has been described as a genocide, Duran (2006, p, 16) noted that between '1870 and 1900, at least 80% of the population had been systematically exterminated'.[16] This occurred in the context of a land-grab to serve a massive influx of European settlers. Native American culture was destroyed but, at the same time, they had difficulty progressing in their new society because of discrimination and perceived inferior status.

American society was based on the concept of a 'melting pot' in which all ethnic groups merge into a common culture. However, this was not a new melange of inputs, but a situation in which ethnic groups were expected to assimilate to the values of the dominant group, In this light, the melting pot has been viewed as a loss of original identity and enforced assimilation.[17]

The United States was not the only nation fostering assimilation, and many of these attempts were done with good, if misguided, intentions. In the British empire, policies were often created to protect indigenous people and help them become 'civilised'. In 1837, the English House of Commons Select Committee on Aborigines was established. Made up of Christian missionaries and government officials, the committee developed assimilation policies for British Commonwealth countries including Canada, Australia and New Zealand. Its focus was on protecting Aborigines from the violence that was occurring on the frontier regions. It advocated the introduction of laws but in a context of assimilating Aborigines into a Christian value system.

In the decades that followed, these governments introduced policies to facilitate assimilation. Between 1869 and 1909, Australia introduced a number of statutes to protect Aborigines. Canada introduced the Indian Act in 1876 followed by a number of subsequent laws. In New Zealand, the Native Department was created in 1861, followed by the Native Schools Act in 1867.[18]

The irony is that while the British were expressing their superiority over the Maori and others, they themselves were treated as inferiors by the Chinese. For a long time, China had seen itself as the pinnacle of world civilisation and saw foreigners like the British as barbarians. However, they had not kept up with changes in the world and they maintained a sense of superiority long after it was justified.

It was not just a European characteristic to speak despairingly of other cultures. For example, an early European ship to New Zealand carried a Tahitian priest by the name of Tupaia, and although Maori and Tahitians were both Polynesian people, Tupaia 'tended to patronise Maori and comment adversely on their customs'.[19] This view was supported by the Europeans who had hoped that Tupaia might be able to raise the condition of Maori. As one European noted, Tupaia

> was more adapted to raise the New Zeelanders [*sic*] to a state of civilisation similar to that of his own islands, than ourselves, to whom the want of the intermediate links, which connect their narrow views to our extended sphere of knowledge, must prove an obstacle in such an undertaking.[20]

Of interest about this note is the European desire to raise the standards of the Maori not by imposing European standards but those of Tahiti. In other words, they thought that one Polynesian culture was better than another.

Ironically, some Maori also expressed similar sentiments when observing other cultures. Te Pahi had the opportunity to visit Sydney and was not impressed by the Australian aboriginals, expressing 'the utmost abhorrence at their going naked, and their want of ingenuity or inclination to produce food and make themselves comfortable'.[21]

It may be that such cultural comparisons are a natural human phenomenon. If a culture embeds its members with values and behaviours that are seen as important, a culture that does not act with those values will naturally be seen as inferior. Psychological processes may also feed this. Psychologists have noted that humans engage in self enhancement and one way this is done through social comparison, that is, comparing themselves to others. However, to state that all negative comments are driven by bias is naïve. Some cultures do provide greater material welfare to their members than others.

A European missionary who had a significant impact on Maori culture was the Reverend Samuel Marsden. His letter to the Church Missionary Society captures many of the characteristics of colonisation and assimilation:

> Having an ardent wish, that the New Zealanders may enjoy the Sweets of Civilisation, and more estimable Blessings of divine Revelation; I shall feel a peculiar Pleasure in seconding any Attempt the Society might be inclined to make for general improvement and advantage.[22]

There is clearly an element of missionary zeal and cultural superiority in this comment. This can be interpreted as arrogant and self-serving in that a missionary imposes his world views on others, but it would be wrong to see this attitude purely in those terms. It also reflects a genuine desire to improve the welfare and life quality of Maori.

And it seems that many Maori shared his view. Maori who visited European settlements acknowledged the gap in prosperity and were keen to acquire European capabilities. For example, when Te Pahi visited Samuel Marsden in Sydney and was shown European rope production techniques, Marsden noted that he wept and exclaimed 'New Zealand was no good'.

When he returned to New Zealand, Te Pahi was 'anxious to introduce the customs and arts of the English' to his people.[23] Te Pahi was just one of many Maori who were 'very desirous to learn the European Arts'.[24]

There is no doubt that a lift in material standards could occur if these ethnic groups assimilated a Western socio-economic system; however, material wealth is only one measure of welfare. If the change in economic system results in a loss of spiritual or social welfare, the net result may be a loss of welfare. Similarly, if it results in an unequal distribution of the 'benefits' from material growth, this can lead to a loss of status and self-esteem. Consequently, this process of imitating the 'superior' culture lost favour, particularly in those nations where assimilation was forced onto ethnic groups.

Assimilation became a 'dirty word' as policy-makers and researchers acknowledged that not everyone wanted to buy into Western culture or, if they did, they wanted to do it on their own terms.[25] For example, Native Americans resisted the idea of enforced assimilation. The expressed feeling was that 'Indians do not desire to be assimilated, and that assimilation is not necessary for Indian progress and participation.'[26]

Assimilation was criticised for its notion of superiority, arrogance and a lack of cultural understanding. In response, multiculturalism was promoted. The term 'multiculturalism' first appeared in the late 1970s and grew in popularity during the 1980s.[27] Multiculturalism signified tolerance and a rejection of discrimination. It was an antidote to a sense of superiority among Western nations, and the view that other cultures were inferior or uncivilised.[28] A multicultural perspective respected alternative views.

The study of economics and culture

While many social scientists were turning against the idea that any culture could have advantages over others, many economists and business specialists were moving in the opposite direction. They became interested in culture in the 1970s as the Japanese powered ahead in many industries the West had pioneered. Much of their success was attributed to aspects of Japanese culture.

When other East Asian 'tigers' followed in Japan's wake, economists embraced cultural explanations for their success in creating wealth. Shared features of East Asian cultures included a respect for education. East Asians also had respect for the role of government while government officials had a responsibility for the common people. This could be traced to the historical concept of 'mandate of heaven' in which rulers lost their right to rule if they failed to serve their people. The persistence of village life in East Asia helped develop a sense of togetherness and ability to work together in confidence. This was claimed to help modern organisations function. Finally, their agricultural resource base required East Asians to adopt values such as thrift and hard work.

Economists began to see culture as an important feature in determining economic growth and welfare. Harvard professor Michael Porter recognised this in his landmark *Competitive Advantage of Nations* in which he recognised that:

> Competitive advantage is created and sustained through a highly localised process. Differences in national economic structures, values, cultures, institutes and histories contribute profoundly to competitive success.[29]

There is no end of examples of the importance of culture for the creation of wealth (and hence the removal of poverty). One of the best documented examples is that of ethnic Chinese in South-East Asia.[30] Despite being a tiny minority, ethnic Chinese dominated the economies of Thailand, the Philippines, Indonesia and Malaysia to a point where some of those governments introduced discriminatory policies against the Chinese.

In Singapore, the prime minister Lee Kuan Yew introduced policies to try to improve the performance of ethnic Malays because at school (and economically) they were falling far behind the ethnic Chinese.[31] This led to the creation of Mendaki (Majlis Pendidikan Anak-Anak Islam – Council on Education for Muslim Children) with the purpose of improving educational outcomes.

Interesting, a culture that at one time facilitates growth can actually be a barrier to growth at other times. For example, Iberian nations built great trading empires in the fifteenth and sixteenth centuries on the basis of a culture characterised by Gold, God and Glory.[32] However, in the seventeenth century wealth creation was more likely to occur through industry and the old culture proved a barrier to adopting the new ways. For example, industry was strongly linked to Jews, and the Christian values that so inspired the Iberians meant that such activity was seen as being below them. It was not consistent with the values of a gentleman (or *hidalgo*).

It was the Dutch that took the lead in the new economy. Simon Schama (1987) described Dutch society as a 'flood society' and only through hard work and with God's help could the Dutch overcome the forces of nature, but if they displayed too much gluttony, vanity and sin, divine wrath would punish them.[33] This created a culture with a strong work ethic and self-regulation. When combined with the high levels of literacy, it was a culture well endowed for the creation of wealth through industry.

Culture can influence economic growth (and the consequent level of wealth) in a number of ways. A culture's values can influence what people want to do. A culture's skill set is an important factor determining what they can do, while the norms and rules influence how they do it. If these factors are consistent with the requirements for economic growth, wealth is more likely to be created.

This view is consistent with the work of institutional economists who have produced a large body of research showing that the motives, values, capabilities and institutions of a culture can have a huge impact on the level of material prosperity. Any culture is strongly shaped by its resource base and the technologies it uses to exploit those resources. Institutional relationships are created that help to maximise production technologies, and those processes become embedded in the culture.

Success in exploiting a production technology is likely to depend on the co-ordinated actions of many individuals. Economic organisations must co-ordinate the activities of a large number of individuals towards the common goal while maintaining motivation. Hence the rules, values and incentives are important to a culture regardless of its productive level. Rules, norms and values all provide the incentive structure of an economy, telling members how to direct their economic activity.[34] They also reflect what is considered rational behaviour within a culture.

Economists found that the nature of incentives, rules, institutions and values plays an important role in determining the level of poverty or prosperity.[35] Hence, cultures are not economically neutral in their ability to produce material wealth. Acknowledging this is essential for understanding and solving poverty.

Herein lies a problem – if we accept that some cultures have advantages in their production of wealth and alleviation of poverty, it would make sense to teach ethnic groups those cultural aspects that can alleviate poverty. However, this runs the danger of returning to the bad old days of assimilation. To avoid this situation, it is necessary to give people freedom to choose. Enforced change can reduce welfare and can be counter-productive. No cultural change should be forced upon a people and no solution advocated in this book should be attempted without the will of the people.

Other explanations for poverty

There are limits to the cultural trauma explanation of poverty. The first is that the ethnic groups suffering from poverty have very different histories. According to the literature on colonial trauma history matters, as David Lloyd notes:

> In the case of colonialism, the relationship to the past is strictly not a relation to one's own past but to a social history and its material and institutional effects and in no simple way a matter of psychic dynamics.[36]

However, the use of cultural trauma has been selective in its use of history, in that it fails to consider the history of the people before colonisation and whether traditional cultures may have also impacted on their current position.

There are also significant differences in the history of ethnic groups that share common economic outcomes. For example, African Americans were not colonised as such, but endured significant injustice. Kidnapped, forced to emigrate and enslaved, they suffered significant discrimination. Assimilation was forced upon them but in a position that would not enable them to make the most of the Western economic system. Forced to conform to the new social structure, most of their old African culture was lost, and they adopted an English-speaking subculture in their new society.[37]

Other groups have not been as badly treated, but claim to suffer cultural trauma through land-loss or loss of social structures, but this leads to another problem, that is identifying how long the inter-generation affects last before adaptation occurs. For example, Scots who suffered in the Highland clearances experienced the same loss of land as Maori but seem to have recovered.

While the poverty of some ethnic groups is attributed to the effect of colonisation, many ethnic groups who haven't experienced colonisation are also suffering from relative poverty and socio-economic marginalisation. Many poorer ethnic groups actually chose to emigrate into a dominant culture that was different from their own. In such instances, cultural trauma fails to provide an explanation. For example, the Spanish Americans who settled in New Mexico were voluntary immigrants. Oliver LaFarge notes that 'They came to plant and maintain the sub-culture of Spain in a new land and not to merge themselves into an English-speaking nation.'[38] They openly opposed assimilation in the new society. Twenty years later, Chiswick (1978) noted that Mexican Americans were poorer than white Americans and the earnings gap remained over successive generations.[39]

In the twenty-first century, Rivera-Batiz (2007) noted that Latin and Caribbean immigrants have higher unemployment rates and earned a wage 54.7% lower than other immigrants.[40] The authors linked this outcome to the immigrant's lower educational attainments, low levels of English-language competence and the decline of US manufacturing which reduced demand for less skilled workers and shifted demand to those with higher skills.

In Germany, Turkish immigrants are disproportionately found in lower socio-economic positions. Such has been their lack of integration that Chancellor Angela Merkel declared 'This [multicultural] approach has failed, utterly failed.' She stressed the importance of learning German and school success to take advantage of opportunities in the labour market.[41]

In Israel, Ethiopian immigrants have high rates of unemployment and welfare dependency. Senor and Singer (2011) state the result is 'an enormous economic burden for Israel'.[42] The immigrants came from an agrarian country with little technology and most did not know how to read or write. Their experience contrasts dramatically with immigrants to Israel from Russia, many of whom had capabilities in the hard sciences and helped fuel a technological boom.

For all its criticism, some level of assimilation may be necessary for socio-economic success and avoiding the development of ethnically defined underclasses. Some localised knowledge and skills are necessary for socio-economic success. Most important is language mastery, which is recognised as an important indicator and prerequisite for social integration.[43] Kristen et al. (2011) state it is one of the most crucial primary ethnic effects and its impact for immigrants' educational success is largely undisputed.[44]

The preceding groups of people voluntarily chose to immigrate to the country in which they are experiencing poorer economic performance. If colonial trauma is the explanation for poverty, these groups should not be doing so badly as they were not colonised.

Discrimination might provide an alternative explanation but if that is the case, why do ethnic minorities continue to immigrate to Western societies? Given that their migration is voluntary, it might be that their relative poverty is something they aspire to and is better than the situation they left behind. It also raises the question as to whether they lacked the capabilities and behaviours necessary to generate higher levels of wealth.

The diversity of experience among ethnic groups shows us that there is no one pattern to poverty. Hence, researchers should be open to diverse causes and solutions. Some people may perpetually be in poverty while some may only endure episodes. For example, Stevens (1999) has shown that the middle classes are now vulnerable to episodes of poverty.[45] However, some groups have characteristics that make them extremely vulnerable and consequently, become an underclass. These characteristics in the right combination could be re-defined as a recipe.

Clydesdale (2017) provided an explanation of how a migrant group might exhibit characteristics that means it is more likely to experience poverty without any discrimination or negative treatment.[46] His focus was on Pacific Island immigrants to New Zealand with whom a number of factors were at play. The first determinant of where people end up in life is where they start. Children born into the upper echelons of society are recipients of many social and economic advantages. These can provide a substantial buffer to hardship.[47] However, Pacific children are not born with these advantages and are more exposed to life's hardships. Of course, they are not the only people in this position as most people are not born into the upper echelons. This is an important ingredient of poverty but, to become an underclass, other factors must work in combination.

A second contributing factor (or ingredient) is the age of the parents when children are born. If the parents are young, they will have had less time to acquire assets and pay off any debt, and because they are early in their careers, they will have lower incomes while trying to raise a family. These disadvantages can set off a cascade of further problems that continue as their family grows. With this in mind, it is worth noting that the average age of Pacific mothers is 25.91 years, while the average age for Europeans is 31.14 years.[48]

A third ingredient is family size. Children cost money and the more children a family has, the greater the financial burden for the parents. With this in mind, Pacific parents carry a greater financial burden than other New Zealanders. On average, they will have 3.2 children compared to the national average of 2.[49] There is a large body of international evidence showing larger families are more likely to endure poverty.[50] Their high expenditure needs also leaves them vulnerable to periods of economic downturn.

Family size also increases the chance that poverty will be carried forward into the next generation. Children from large families are less likely to be educated and receive nutrition adequate for normal development.[51] Not surprisingly, New Zealand statistics reveal that between 1984 and 2012, those households with three or more children experienced poverty at rates consistently higher than those that only had one or two children.[52]

The final ingredient is low income. Pacific Islanders are disproportionately found in low-paid jobs. Statistics on Pacific immigrants over the age of 30 found that 38.4% work as machinery operators, drivers and labourers. The figure for other immigrants is 8.8%. By contrast only 10.2% of non-Pacific immigrants work in these low-skilled professions.[53] Few Pacific immigrants obtain professional positions. Only 13.9% of Pacific immigrants above the age of 30 obtained managerial/professional positions. The corresponding figure for non-Pacific immigrants is 52.1%. For immigrants under the age of 30, the figures are 37.1%.

The differences in vocation and income are reflected the categories by which immigrants gain entry into New Zealand. They are less likely to enter the country under the skilled/business category. For immigrants above the age of 30, only 15.5% entered under these professional categories. This compares to 65.5% for other immigrants. However, if considering culture, the Pacific figure may be inflated as it includes Fijian Indians. If an attempt is made to isolate those of Polynesian culture, only 9.7% of Tongans enter under the skilled business category. For Samoans, the figure is 0.0%.[54]

If the culture believes that a woman's place is in the home, this too can reduce family income. The same affect can occur if they have more children as mothers need to be home more where they will not be earning a wage. Notably, the employment and labour participation rates for Pacific women are 10% and 15% below non-Pacific immigrants.[55] The rates for Pacific men are only slightly lower than other ethnic groups but the overall consequence is Pacific immigrants have a lower labour participation and employment rate, and are more likely to be characterised as single-income families.

Pacific families in New Zealand are more likely to be characterised by all of these features and have emerged into a category that sociologists have called an underclass. Their parents have families at a younger age and hence have fewer resources. They are more likely to be single-income families, and because their jobs are low-skilled, they are likely to be low incomes. At the same time, expenditure is likely to be higher because of the higher number of children. These ingredients mean that Pacific people have a strong propensity towards poverty. Consequently, the Ministry of Social Development notes that being from the Pacific 'increased the likelihood of experiencing severe or significant poverty and hardship'.[56]

However, it should not be assumed that those under the poverty line will always be there. In a US study, Stevens (1999) noted that poverty can actually be a temporary phenomenon.[57] A family or individual may be impoverished for a number of years then see their circumstances improve, perhaps by gaining a well-paying job. They may enjoy this situation for several years but then another life change results in them falling back into poverty.

Stevens noted the problem for low-income families is that, although they manage to escape poverty in good times, they do not rise much above the poverty line.[58] This leaves them vulnerable to detrimental economic events that can push them back into a position of extreme hardship, So, although not perpetually in a state of poverty, they can experience several long periods of hardship, Their marginal position and low skill-base make them particularly vulnerable to business cycles.

In summary, a number of characteristics of an ethnic group, working in concert, could lend themselves to poverty. It might be expected that some of these characteristics would change in subsequent generations. For example, we might expect the next generation to have better English skills, achieve more relevant education in their new country and thereby earn better incomes. However, many ethnic groups remain with lower educational outcomes and low-income employment. Given the diversity of experiences, researchers need to expand the range of explanations considered and leave no stone un-turned in pursuit of solutions.

Notes

1 Lewis, O. (1959). *Five Families: Mexican Case Studies in the Culture of Poverty. With a Foreword by Oliver La Farge.* New York: Basic Books.
2 Lewis, O. (1969). The culture of poverty. In D.P. Moynihan (Ed.), *On Understanding Poverty: Perspectives from the Social Sciences.* New York: Basic Books, p. 188.
3 Ibid., p. 196.
4 Lewis, O. (1998). The culture of poverty. *Society, 35*(2), 7–9, p. 7.
5 Lewis (1969), p. 188.
6 Kurtz, D.V. (2014). Culture, poverty, politics: Cultural sociologists, Oscar Lewis, Antonio Gramsci. *Critique of Anthropology, 34*(3), 327–345.
7 Small, M.L., Harding, D.J. & Lamont, M. (2010). Introduction. Reconsidering Culture and Poverty. Special Issue. *The ANNALS of the American Academy of Political and Social Science, 629*(1), 6–27.
8 Ryan, W. (1976). *Blaming the Victim.* Revised edition. New York: Vintage Books.
9 Small, Harding, & Lamont (2010).
10 Stack, C.B. (1974). *Strategies for Survival in a Black Community.* New York: Harper & Row.
11 Patterson, O. (2000). Taking culture seriously: A framework and an Afro-American illustration. In Harrison, L.E., & Huntington, S.P (Eds.), *Culture Matters: How Values Shape Human Progress.* New York: Basic Books.
12 Small, Harding, & Lamont (2010), p. 8.
13 Lloyd, D. (2000). Colonial trauma/postcolonial recovery? *Interventions, 2*(2), 212–228.
14 Reid, J., Taylor-Moore, K., & Varona, G. (2014). Towards a social-structural model for understanding current disparities in Maori health and well-being. *Journal of Loss and Trauma, 19*(6), 514–536.
15 Lewis (1969), p. 188.
16 Duran, E. (2006). *Healing the Soul Wound: Counselling with American Indians and Other Native Peoples.* New York: Teachers College Press, p. 16.
17 La Farge, O. (1956). Assimilation: The Indian view. *New Mexico Quarterly, 26*(1), 5–13, p. 7.
18 Armitage, A. (1995). *Comparing the Policy of Aboriginal Assimilation: Australia, Canada, and New Zealand.* Vancouver BC: UBC Press.
19 Salmond, A. (1997) *Between Worlds: Early Exchanges between Maori and Europeans 1773–1815.* Auckland: Viking, p. 91.
20 Ibid.
21 Cited in Salmond (1997), p. 351.
22 Marsden to Pratt, 24 March 1808, in Marsden, S., Pratt, J., & Havard-Williams, P. (1961). *Marsden and the New Zealand Mission: Sixteen Letters.* University of Otago Press in association with AH and AW Reed, pp. 13–14.
23 Cited in Salmond (1997), p. 358.
24 Kendell's observation of Hongi Hika cited in Salmond (1997), p. 438.
25 Roberts, S. (2008). In a generation, minorities may be the U.S. majority. *New York Times*, 14 August; La Farge (1956).
26 La Farge (1956), p. 10.
27 Reisch, M. (2008). From melting pot to multiculturalism: The impact of racial and ethnic diversity on social work and social justice in the USA. *British Journal of Social Work*, 38(4), 788–804.
28 Tuhiwai-Smith, L. (1999). *Decolonizing Methodologies: Research and Indigenous Peoples.* London and New York: Zed Books.
29 Porter, M. (1990). *The Competitive Advantage of Nations.* Basingstoke: Macmillan, p. 19.
30 Clydesdale, G. (2017). *The Art of Business: How the Chinese Got Rich.* London: Robinson.

31 Yew, L.K. (2012). *From Third World to First: The Singapore Story, 1965–2000.* New York: Harper Collins.
32 Clydesdale, G. (2016). *Waves of Prosperity.* London: Robinson.
33 Schama, S. (1988). *The Embarrassment of Riches: An Interpretation of Dutch Culture in the Golden Age.* Berkeley: University of California Press.
34 Boland, L.A. (1979). Knowledge and the role of institutions in economic theory. *Journal of Economic Issues, 13*(4), 957–972; Johnson, B. (1992). Institutional learning, in B.A. Lundvall (Ed,), *National Innovation System: Towards a Theory of Innovation and Interactive Learning.* London: Pinter.
35 North, D. (1990). *Institutions, Institutional Change and Economic Performance.* Cambridge: Cambridge University Press, p. 25; Johnson (1992), p. 26.
36 Lloyd (2000), p. 216.
37 La Farge (1956).
38 LaFarge (1956), p. 11.
39 Chiswick, B.R. (1978). The effect of Americanization on the earnings of foreign-born men. *Journal of Political Economy*, 86, 897–921.
40 Rivera-Batiz, F.L. (2007). How do migrants from Latin America and the Caribbean fare in the US labour market? *The World Economy, 30*, 1399–1429.
41 Weaver, M. (2010). Angela Merkel: German multiculturalism has 'utterly failed', *The Guardian*, Sunday 17 October.
42 Senor, D., & Singer, S. (2009). *Start-up Nation: The Story of Israel's Economic Miracle.* New York: Twelve, p. 123.
43 Esser, H. (2006). *Sprache und Integration: Die sozialen Bedingungen und Folgen des Spracherwerbs von Migranten.* Frankfurt A. M.: Campus Verlag.
44 Kristen, C., Edele, D.P.A., Kalter, F., Kogan, I., Schulz, B., Stanat, P., & Will, D.P.G. (2011). The education of migrants and their children across the life course. *Zeitschrift für Erziehungswissenschaft, 14*, 121–137.
45 Stevens, A.H. (1999). Climbing out of poverty, falling back in: Measuring the persistence of poverty over multiple spells. *The Journal of Human Resources*, 34, 557–588.
46 Clydesdale, G. (2017). *The Politically Correct Economy.* Christchurch: Craft Publications.
47 McNamee, S., & Miller, R. (2004). *The Meritocracy Myth.* Lanham, MD: Rowman & Littlefield.
48 StatisticsNZ (2006). *Census Data.* Wellington: Statistics New Zealand.
49 Ministry of Pacific Island Affairs (2002). *Pacific Progress: A Report on the Economic Status of Pacific Peoples in New Zealand.* Wellington: Statistics New Zealand.
50 Bauer, J., Canlas, D., Fernandez, M.T., & Mason, A. (1992). *Family Size and Family Welfare in the Philippines.* East-West Center Working Papers, Population Series, No. 67, Honolulu: East-West Center. Illarionov, A., Layard, R., & Orszag, P. (1993). *The Conditions of Life.* Working Paper No. 414, London: London School of Economics.
51 Bauer et al. (1992).
52 Office of Children's Commissioner (2013) *Child Poverty Monitor.* Technical Report, Office of Children's Commissioner. Downloaded from http://www.nzchildren.co.nz/document_downloads/2013%20Child%20Poverty%20Monitor%20Technical%20Report%20MASTER.pdf.
53 Bedford, R., Masgoret, A.M, Tausi, M., & Merwood, P. (2008). Immigrants from the Pacific: 'drain on the economy' or active participation in the labour force? Paper presented at the 13th International Metropolis Conference, World Conference Centre, Bonn, 27–31 October.
54 Ibid.
55 Ibid.
56 The Ministry of Social Development (2008), p. 4.
57 Stevens (1999).
58 Ibid.

3 What is the link between culture and economic systems?

There is a long-established academic literature linking culture and economic outcomes. One of the earliest is Weber's *The Protestant Ethic and the Spirit of Capitalism* which focused on the origins of modern society and the emergence of Western capitalism.[1] Weber argued that the Protestant religion possessed an ethos and values that contributed to economic growth. The problem with this view was that functional equivalents of Protestantism have been found in other religions that Weber did not believe facilitated growth.[2]

However, if we move from values and ethos to actual behaviours, Weber's views may have more merit. Weber argued that Protestantism, in particular its Calvinist forms, promoted behaviours conducive to economic growth. That is, hard work, honesty, seriousness and the thrifty use of money. Protestantism did not actually promote the pursuit of wealth, but encouraged behaviours from which wealth was a consequence.

David Landes (2000) identified two other characteristics of Protestants.[3] First is their high level of literacy, a by-product of Bible reading (by contrast, Catholics were not expected to read the Bible) and second was the importance that Protestants gave to time. This could be seen in the fact that most clockmakers and watchmakers were Protestants, even in Catholic areas. Today we take time for granted, but the concept of measuring time was unique to Europeans. Other people were aware of seasons, lunar cycles and daily rhythms, but no other people measured and planned their lives around time to the same extent.

Many of the characteristics that Weber identified in Protestants could also be found in north-east Asians, especially the Chinese. They too had an emphasis on hard work, seriousness and the thrifty use of money.[4] If culture was a determinant of wealth, they too should be rich, and the historical evidence supports this to be the case. For much of humanity, the Chinese have ranked among the wealthiest nations on the planet.

However, in the Ching dynasty, the Chinese fell behind the West. Much of this can be attributed to the nature of the economic system that developed in China, and it is notable that when Chinese left that system and migrated to British colonies, the Chinese continued to build wealth.[5] However, there is one other cultural development which contributed to the gap between China and the West, and that is the greater use of knowledge, science and technology.

From the eighteenth century and the industrial revolution, Europeans made more extensive use of knowledge, science and technology to improve industry and welfare. Mokyr (2005) believes the industrial revolution that occurred in Britain was born on the back of the Enlightenment which increased the amount of knowledge.[6] That knowledge also became more accessible for those who could use it. He states:

> The short answer as to why the West is so much richer today than it was two centuries ago is that collectively, these societies "know" more ... Greater specialisation, professionalism, and expertization have meant that the total amount of knowledge that society controls is vastly larger than ever before.[7]

During the Enlightenment, European thinkers developed a more systematic pursuit of knowledge and analysis. Most innovators in the early years were best described as 'tinkerers' not scientists,[8] but by the nineteenth century, the connection between science and technology had become tighter. More books were published to store this knowledge and a spread in literacy helped promote accessibility to that knowledge. This was complemented by an increase in the number of institutions conducting research and advancing knowledge.

The Enlightenment was a knowledge revolution. Mokyr notes that 'nothing of this sort, I submit, can be detected at this time in the Ottoman empire, Japan, India, Africa or China'.[9] The Enlightenment and scientific revolution paved the way for a knowledge economy which transformed business. This could be seen in the United States where Charles Schwab, the founder of US Steel, noted that American industrial leadership was won by transforming the raw materials of the earth in a 'scientific manner'.[10] Clydesdale (2017) compared the West to the Chinese who continued to practise the 'art of business'.[11] By contrast, Westerners increasingly practised the 'science of business'.

The development of a knowledge economy significantly raised prosperity levels, hence when Westerners travelled the world and observed other groups, they were well aware of their material superiority. But their observation suffered from bias in that the measure of wealth depends on the position of the observer. If there is a natural state of material wealth, it was the poorer nations who more accurately represented how the vast majority of humans had lived. This so-called poverty was not the abnormality – Western wealth was.

The levels of wealth found in the West do not exist in nature but must be created. To create such wealth, high levels of knowledge and cognitive skills are needed and this, in turn, would lead to changes in education, parenting and culture.

Karl Marx also identified a link between culture and economics. In contrast to Weber who claimed that culture determines economic outcomes, Karl Marx noted causality works the other way. In Marx's eyes, a society's resource base determines the culture. In his famous quote from the *Poverty of Philosophy*, Marx noted that the 'hand-mill gives you society with the feudal lord; the steam-mill society with the industrial capitalist'.[12]

In *A Contribution to the Critique of Political Economy*, Marx wrote that a society's structure was linked to the development of their 'material productive forces'. He noted that 'The mode of production of material life conditions the social, political and intellectual life process in general.'[13] His writings focused on relations in society, but within his comment is the acknowledgement that the economic resource base determines behaviours in a culture.

Beyond relations, the resource base also determines what resources are used and what capabilities are developed to exploit those resources. For example, a resource base consisting of flax enables a culture in which clothes, baskets, hunting traps and other artefacts are made of that resource, but it requires members to develop capabilities in flax-weaving. Similarly, people living on an isolated island are likely to develop skills in fishing.

The skills of the parents play a large role in what is passed on to their children, whether it is fishing or flax-weaving. It is the same in a developed market economy. Even though formal education plays a major role, the skills of the parents will significantly determine what is passed on to their children.

Many people reading this will argue that this is a highly materialistic view of culture, and understates the importance of the spiritual. However, much of what we consider spiritual also has its basis in the economic. It was the anthropologist Malinowski who first noted this.[14] Malinowski studied the lives of Trobiand islanders of the Pacific Ocean. Much of their economic output came from working in the garden. Hence, Malinowski noted 'Half of the natives' working life is spent in the garden, and around it centres perhaps more than half of his interests and ambitions.' In Malinowski's description of garden work, we can see the link between the spiritual and the economic. He notes that the garden magician

> has to perform a series of rites and spells over the garden, which run parallel with the labour, and which, in fact, initiate each stage of the work and each new development of the plant life. Even before any gardening is begun at all, the magician has to consecrate the site with a big ceremonial performance in which all the men of the village take part. This ceremony officially opens the season's gardening, and only after it is performed do the villagers begin to cut the scrub on their plots. Then, in a series of rites, the magician inaugurates successively all the various stages which follow one another—the burning of the scrub, the clearing, the planting, the weeding and the harvesting …
>
> The garden magician, according to native ideas, thus controls both the work of man and the forces of Nature. He also acts directly as supervisor of gardening, sees to it that people do not skimp their work, or lag behind with it. Thus magic is a systematising, regulating, and controlling influence in garden work. The magician, in carrying out the rites, sets the pace, compels people to apply themselves to certain tasks, and to accomplish them properly and in time … there is no doubt that by its influence in ordering, systematising and regulating work, magic is economically invaluable for the natives.[15]

Given the high value placed on this resource utilisation, it became an important source of self-esteem for the Trobiand islander. Malinowski notes that:

> A good garden worker in the Trobriands derives a direct prestige from the amount of labour he can do, and the size of garden he can till. The title *tokwaybagula*, which means "good" or "efficient gardener," is bestowed with discrimination, and borne with pride. Several of my friends, renowned as *tokwaybagula*, would boast to me how long they worked, how much ground they tilled, and would compare their efforts with those of less efficient men … Men vie with one another in their speed, in their thoroughness, and in the weights they can lift, when bringing big poles to the garden, or in carrying away the harvested yams.[16]

It would be wrong to attribute all garden behaviour to utilitarian values. Malinowski stresses that behaviour was driven by many complex social and traditional motives. Nevertheless, it is clear from his description that even magical, religious and superstitious behaviours have their basis in the society's resource base. He noted there was a 'constant economic undertow to all public and private life'.[17] Rites, ceremonies and rules had an economic purpose in maximising the island's resource use.

We think of priests as protecting spiritual welfare, but they also played an important role protecting material welfare. With the advent of agriculture, priests played a prime role in the economy. In agricultural societies, a number of dangers could undermine prosperity and security. These threats came from droughts, floods, parasites, weeds and soil depletion. Human threats included the arrival of hostile groups who could steal and destroy crops and food stores. It wasn't just invaders who could cause concern. A harvest could fail as a result of faulty sowing, nursing, harvesting or storing, while food stores might not last as a result of negligence, ignorance or greed. In such circumstances, society needed someone to manage the relationship with the environment and impose discipline on society. It is here that priests proved their economic worth.

Priests possessed the knowledge of plants and animals, and the conditions that influenced their growth. They also mediated with the supernatural world, in an attempt to manage the weather, seasons, parasites and pests. Priests often had the task of timing and maintenance of the agricultural calendar. They advised peasants when to till the land, sow, weed, harvest or break into winter stocks.[18]

Priests were also responsible for ensuring people operated with self-restraint. They imposed discipline on the populace to ensure they worked hard, stored stocks wisely, and distributed food in a manner that was fair and sustainable. This increased the chance that society could survive periods of scarcity. Without this restriction on human behaviour, we could expect the strongest members of the community to seize the best food stocks or, alternatively, feast until nothing remained. Community feasts were allowed and led by the priests, but after a few days of feasting the frugal times began again. Priests led rites of harvest and slaughter in which people committed themselves to a greater discipline, even though they were surrounded by a springtime harvest.

The link between the spiritual and economic is prevalent in cultures around the world, and can even be seen in the Judeo-Christian tradition. Many of the laws contained in the first five books of the Bible govern production and consumption. For example, Exodus 23 advises peasants to rest their land every seventh year to avoid depleting the soil.

> For six years you are to sow your fields and harvest the crops, but during the seventh year let the land lie un-ploughed and un-used. Then the poor among your people may get food from it, and the wild animals may eat what they leave. Do the same with your vineyard and olive grove.[19]

Trade was also covered. Levitical courts supervised weights and measures, and from the third century, rabbinical courts were granted control over monetary issues and private property. The book of Leviticus also gave instruction on honest business practices. Customers should not be over-charged or underpaid:

> And if thou sell ought unto thy neighbour, or buyest (ought) of thy neighbour's hand, ye shall not oppress one another ...[20]

The laws were not restricted to production and trade. Laws were also laid down for consumption, most notably a dietary system known as the 'kashrut'. The most detailed description of this system is found in Leviticus chapter 11, which lists those animals that can and cannot be eaten. For example, it states that animals that chew their cud can be eaten as can those with a split hoof, like cattle and lamb. However, animals that don't chew their cud should not be eaten, nor those that don't have a split hoof, like rabbits and pigs.

At the core of all these relations was the economic relationship that the Jews had with their God. They had formed a contract, a covenant with their God, in which they agreed to worship their God and obey his rules. In return, he offered resources and prosperity:

> If you pay heed to the commandments which I give you this day, and love the Lord your God and serve him with all your heart and soul, then I will send rain for your land in season ... and you will gather your corn and new wine and oil, and I will provide pasture ... you will eat your fill.
>
> Take care not to be led astray in your hearts nor to turn aside and serve other gods ... or the Lord will become angry with you: he will shut up the skies and there will be no rain, your ground will not yield its harvest, and you will soon vanish from the rich land which the Lord is giving you.[21]

This chapter has revealed that the resource base has a huge influence on people's values, motivations and beliefs. It also determines the capabilities needed to prosper with those resources. In the next chapter, we will note the important role that parents play imparting these capabilities to their children.

Notes

1 Weber, M. (2002, 1920). *The Protestant Ethic and the Spirit of Capitalism: And Other Writings*. London: Penguin.
2 Swidler, A. (1986). Culture in action: Symbols and strategies. *American Sociological Review*, 51(2), 273–286.
3 Landes, D. (2000). Culture makes almost all the difference. In L.E. Harrison and S.P. Huntington (Eds.), *Culture Matters: How Values Shape Human Progress*. New York: Basic Books, pp. 2–13.
4 Clydesdale, G. (2017). *The Art of Business*. London: Robinson.
5 Ibid.
6 Mokyr, J. (2005). The intellectual origins of modern economic growth. *The Journal of Economic History, 65*(2), 285–351.
7 Ibid., p. 287.
8 Clydesdale, G. (2016). *Waves of Prosperity: India, China and the West*. London: Robinson.
9 Mokyr (2005), p. 323.
10 Clydesdale (2016), p. 266.
11 Clydesdale (2017).
12 Marx, K. (1976, 1847). The poverty of philosophy. In *Marx-Engels Collected Works: Volume 6: Marx and Engels, 1845–1848*. New York: International Publishers.
13 Marx, K. (1979, 1859). Preface to *A Contribution to the Critique of Political Economy*. London: Maurice Dobb.
14 Malinowski, B. (1922). *Argonauts of the Western Pacific: An Account of Native Enterprise and Adventure in the Archipelagoes of Melanesian New Guinea*. London: George Routledge and Sons; New York: E. P. Dutton and Co. Downloaded from: http://www.bohol.ph/books/Argonauts/Argonauts.html#d0e2287.
15 Ibid., pp. 59–60.
16 Ibid., p. 61.
17 Ibid., p. 8.
18 Goudsblom, J. (1996). Ecological regimes and the rise of organised religion. In J. Goudsblom, E.L. Jones, & S. Mennell (Eds.), *The Course of Human History: Economic Growth Social Process and Civilization*. New York: M.E. Sharpe, pp. 31–48.
19 Exodus 23.
20 Leviticus 25:14.
21 Deuteronomy 11:13–17.

4 What is the link between culture, parenting and children's ability?

> Give me a child until he is seven and I will give you the man.
>
> Jesuit Motto

Anthropologists have long realised the link between parenting, culture and education. As Harkness and Super note 'Parenting is culturally constructed ... parents in different cultures receive many different kinds of guidance about how to rear children properly, whether in the form of books, of advice or simply in training by example.'[1]

Margaret Mead pioneered work in this area in her book *Growing Up in New Guinea*, and lesser so in *Coming of Age in Samoa.* [2] Mead's description of child and family life in Pacific Island tribes opened up a new form of study which detailed the relationship between child development, the role of parents and its relationship with culture.

Mead observed the role that parents played in educating children for their future life and also, how the environment shaped parental behaviour. For example, the following statement records how children in the Manus Islands were trained to prepare for life in a marine environment. She begins: 'The Manus baby is accustomed to water from the first years of his life.' Mead then goes on to describe learning in this environment. For example, the child must learn how to hold on to his mother when travelling by canoe:

> When he is about a year old, he has learned to grasp his mother firmly around the throat, so that he can ride in safety, poised on the back of her neck ... The decisive angry gesture with which he was re-seated on his mother's neck whenever his grip tended to slacken has taught him to be alert and sure-handed.[3]
>
> For the first few months after he has begun to accompany his mother about the village the baby rides quietly on her neck or sits in the bow of the canoe while his mother punts in the stern some ten feet away. The child sits quietly schooled by the hazards to which he has been earlier exposed ... If he should tumble over board, there would be no tragedy ... The mother or father is there to pick him up ... so the child confronts duckings falls, dousing of cold water, or entanglements of slimy sea weed ...[4]

It was not just the mother who engaged in training. The following description reveals how the father taught the child to do its own canoeing:

> The next step in water proficiency is reached when the child begins to punt a large canoe. Early in the morning the village is alive with canoes in which the elders sit sedately on the centre platforms while small children of three punt the canoes which are three or four times as long as the children are tall ... The father sits in casual state, a man of five feet nine or ten, weighing a hundred and fifty pounds. The canoe is long and heavy, dug out of a solid log; the unwieldy outrigger makes it difficult to steer. At the end of the long craft, perched precariously on the thin gunwales, his tiny brown feet curved tensely to keep his hold, stands a small brown baby, manfully straining at the six foot punt in his hands. He is so small that he looks more like an unobtrusive stern ornament than like the pilot of the lumbering craft. Slowly, with a great display of energy but not too much actual progress, the canoe moves through the village, among other canoes similarly manned by the merest tots. But this is neither child labour nor idle prestige hunting on the part of the parents. It is part of the whole system by which a child is encouraged to do his physical best.[5]
>
> The test of this kind of training is in the results. The Manus children are perfectly at home in the water. They neither fear it nor regard it as presenting special difficulties and dangers.[6]

The Manus Island mother engaged in the same parental behaviours that we observe in mothers everywhere; that is nurturing, training, control and sociability. As Mead notes, the mothers 'every move is a reassurance to the child'.[7] In Mead's descriptions we observe common parenting behaviour, but it is adapted to the needs of the local environment. The child's

> whole play world is so arranged that he is permitted to make small mistakes from which he may learn better judgement and greater circumspection, but he is never allowed to make mistakes which are serious enough to frighten him permanently or inhibit his activity.[8]

Manus Island parents allowed their children to make mistakes. Allowing children to learn from physical mistakes 'makes children develop perfect motor coordination ... in the everyday activities of swimming, paddling, punting, climbing, there is a general high level of excellence'.[9] Of note in this comment is the emphasis on motor skills, which stands in sharp contrast to the need for cognitive skills in the modern economy.

A common sub-theme of the early anthropological studies is the labelling of child-rearing customs as 'education'.[10] Parents and family elders performed the role of educating children and preparing them for the demands of adult life. In this way, the environment and resource base shaped culture and parental practice. Parents then transmitted these cultural behaviours, values and norms to the child.

Training of this nature, by parents and elders, is a common characteristic of preliterate societies. Middleton (1970) notes that formal education through schooling is only a characteristic of literate societies.[11] This is an important observation as it recognises that different socio-economic systems require different forms of education. The modern economy and technological resource base require skills in literacy, science and technology. The emphasis is on cognitive skills, not motor skills.

The parental emphasis on the children's motor skills, that Mead observed in the Pacific, has also been observed in east Africa. Hence, their children's motor skills are more advanced than those of US children. By contrast, Western children have greater vocabulary and language skills, a reflection of their parent's values. That is not to say that Westerners ignore motor skills nor that East Africans ignore cognitive skills. Parents across societies develop both these capabilities. 'The difference is in the level of a particular behavior, not its existence.'[12]

As far back as 1956, academics have known that infants in Africa infants learn motor skills earlier than American children.[13] It has since been widely investigated by studies that have confirmed these differences.[14] The question is 'is the rapid learning rate of Africans a result of genetics or nurture?' The answer was provided by Charles Super (1976) who examined very young Kipsigis children of Kenya.[15] Through a range of testing, Super confirmed that 'Kipsigis babies were able to sit, stand and walk considerably earlier than their American counterparts'.[16]

He did note that they were not more advanced in all areas of motor development, but in those areas where they were ahead, the role of parental training and nurturing was clear:

> Most mothers in Kokwet (over 80 per cent) deliberately teach their babies to sit, stand and walk, all areas of development in which these children are more advanced than American babies. There are special words in the Kipsigis language for the teaching of sitting and walking, and the methods of teaching are relatively standardized.
>
> ... Teaching to sit usually starts about the fifth or sixth month. The child is set down into a special hole in the ground that has been made to help support his back, or blankets are nestled around him. Such procedures are carried out on most days until the baby can sit quite well.
>
> Another deliberate behavior by the mothers and caretakers is also important for the development of walking. When the baby is about one month old the mother starts to play with the baby in a particular way called kitwalse (literally, "to make jump"). This consists of holding the infant under the arms and bouncing him on one's lap. to which the infant responds with the standing or stepping reflex. Of course, this kind of play is not unique to Kipsigis parents, but it seems to be more frequent than in American families ...[17]

The reference to standardised parenting practices confirms the role of common parental practices in a culture and the targeting of specific capabilities necessary in that society. Most importantly, it confirms the importance placed on motor skills.

Super did not restrict his study to the Kipsigis. His interviews and observations were carried out in twelve other diverse groups in Africa from nomadic Boran peoples who lived in the north-eastern desert to Highland Bantu farmers. He found that although there was significant variation, all groups were more advanced than Americans.

Why do ethnic groups vary in their nurturing?

Anthropologists have built a significant body of information on cultures around the world. They discovered that the practices by which children are reared are strongly influenced by their culture's history and physical environment. This in turn shapes the child's development. For example, Barry, Child and Bacon (1959) explored the link between economic systems and child-rearing.[18] In a cross-cultural study of 104 societies, they rated societies depending on how they acquired food resources. Some economies were based on hunting and gathering in which people engaged in foraging, fishing or hunting. Once acquired, their food was immediately consumed. At the other extreme were economies based on pastoralism or agriculture. Daily activities in these societies involved the tending of animals and crops. Consumption was less immediate. Crops had to be harvested, stored and rationed out over time to last until the next harvest.

The authors found that these daily activities facilitated the socialisation of children. Societies that accumulated food over time needed adults who were responsible, conservative and respectful of elders. Hence, the socialisation of children had a stronger emphasis on obedience and responsibility. However, in economies with more immediate consumption, behaviour was less conservative. These societies needed 'adults who could exercise initiative and imagination in finding food for the day'. Children socialised in these societies were encouraged towards achievement, self-reliance and independence. So consistent were their findings that the authors concluded that:

> a knowledge of the economy alone would enable one to predict with considerable accuracy whether a society's socialization pressures were primarily toward compliance or assertion.[19]

This work has become a classic in anthropology and 'anthropologists do indeed predict (with considerable accuracy) the type of parenting styles that will be encountered in small-scale non-Western, traditional societies'.[20] An example of this is a study of the Kipsigis of Kenya.[21] A high-accumulation society, the researchers found their children were socialised to be responsible and obedient. They were socialised to be responsible for tasks in agriculture, cow herding, food preparation and infant care.

By contrast, the !Kung are a traditional hunting and gathering society and their children had a longer period of infancy and were expected to do little work until adolescence.[22] However, as society transitioned from life in the bush to a sedentary agricultural economy, children were increasingly trained to help out with household work, a reflection of the link between parenting, capabilities and the economy.

The importance of changing parental behaviours as the economic base changes can be seen in a study of Ngecha in Kenya.[23] In the five-year period after gaining independence (1968–1973), the Ngecha underwent rapid social change. It transitioned from an agrarian to a wage-earning economy, with new technologies and modifications in daily routines and living arrangements. The women of the village became important agents of social change. They reconfigured their values and aspirations for their children with success in formal schooling becoming a priority. Interesting, they also modernised their concept of what was considered a 'good child'. Under the traditional agricultural economy, a good child was one who was 'respectful, obedient, generous, and goodhearted'. In the new economy, it became one who was 'clever, inquisitive, confident, brave'. Of course, these changes led to conflict with those holding the values of earlier generations.

John and Beatrice Whiting are recognised as the founders of comparative child development. In the early 1950s, they commenced their Six Culture Study in which they systematically observed children in six different cultures.[24] Their study revealed valuable information on the way that cultural environments affect children's social behaviour. They coined the term *cultural learning environment* which refers to the features of everyday life that set the stage for child development and socialisation. These factors influence the development outcomes for children and include the nature of time spent in play and work, eat and sleep and who they interact with in their community. Parents are seen as socialising agents, creating the setting for development:

> the effect of culture on these patterns in childhood is a direct consequence of the settings to which children are assigned and the people who frequent them. Socializing agents orchestrate children's participation in these learning environments by assigning children to some and proscribing others. Our theory holds that the power of parents and socializers to mold social behavior lies primarily in the assignment of boys and girls to different settings where they interact with different categories of individuals.[25]

Studies from anthropologists show a link between the economic/resource base, culture and parenting. The economic base provides the means of survival which fashions the behaviours, capabilities and values of a culture. This, in turn, influences how parents bring up their children. Whiting and Edwards categorised mothers' behaviour into groupings, that is nurturance, training, control and sociability. All parents engage in these behaviours but how it is done varies within cultures and is strongly shaped by the physical and social setting in which a child lives.[26]

By combining the work of anthropologists with economic historians we are able to answer the questions 'why do ethnic groups vary in their nurturing' and 'why do those differences affect cognitive/intellectual outcomes?' Since the Enlightenment, the West has developed a knowledge economy which has encouraged parents to focus on cognitive skills and academic socialisation. By contrast, traditional societies have continued to focus on motor skills which have more relevance to their environments and resource base.

Parental behaviour lays the foundation for subsequent learning. Consequently, ethnic groups will enter school with varying abilities which reflect the varying focus of their nurturing. Consequently, children of many ethnic groups enter school with lower cognitive, maths and reading scores. Not only does this have implications for their academic and intellectual progress, it contributes to their economic growth.

Finally, we must acknowledge that there is a lot of variation within each ethnic group. For example, many parents in the West show little regard for academic socialisation and cognitive development. Not everyone reads books on parenting. However, much of that knowledge filters down through newspaper articles and inter-parent conversation. Parents acquire this information at different rates. Consequently, advance does not occur at a consistent rate and significant variation exists, even within Western societies.

Notes

1 Harkness, S., & Super, C.M. (2002). Culture and parenting. *Handbook of Parenting, 2*, 253–280, p. 253.
2 Mead, M. (1968, 1928). *Coming of Age in Samoa: A Psychological Study of Primitive Youth for Western Civilization*. New York: Dell; Mead, M. (1966, 1930). *Growing up in New Guinea: A Comparative Study of Primitive Education*. New York: Morrow.
3 Mead (1930/1966), p. 25.
4 Ibid., p. 26.
5 Ibid., p. 29.
6 Ibid., p. 30.
7 Ibid., p. 27.
8 Ibid., pp. 26–7.
9 Ibid., pp. 30–31.
10 Harkness and Super (2002), p. 259.
11 Middleton, J. (Ed.) (1970). *From Child to Adult: Studies in the Anthropology of Education*. New York: Natural History Press.
12 Brooks-Gunn, J., & Markman, L.B. (2005). The contribution of parenting to ethnic and racial gaps in school readiness. *The Future of Children*, 15(1), 139–168.
13 Geber, M. (1956). Développement psycho-moteur de l'enfant africain. *Courrier, 6*(1), 17–29.
14 For example LeVine, R.A. (1970). Cross-cultural study in child psychology. *Carmichael's Manual of Child Psychology, 2*, 559–612; Weyl, N., & Possony, S. (1963) *The Geography of Intellect*. Chicago: Regenery.
15 Super, C.M. (1976). Environmental effects on motor development: The case of 'African infant precocity'. *Developmental Medicine & Child Neurology, 18*(5), 561–567.
16 Ibid., p. 562.
17 Ibid., pp. 562–3.
18 Barry, H.I., Child, I.L., & Bacon, M. K. (1959). Relations of child training to subsistence economy. *American Anthropologist, 61*, 51–63.
19 Barry, H.I, Child, I.L. & Bacon, M.K. (1959). Relations of child training to subsistence economy. In C.S. Ford (Ed.), *Cross-cultural Approaches: Readings in Comparative Research*. New Haven, CT: HRAF Press, p. 254.

20 Harkness & Super (2002), p. 262.

21 Harkness, S., & Super, C.M. (1985). Child–environment interactions in the socialization of affect. In M. Lewis & C. Saarni (Eds.), *The Socialization of Emotions.* New York: Plenum, pp. 21–36. Harkness, S., & Super, C.M. (1991). East Africa. In H.R. Hiner & J.M. Hawes (Eds.), *Children in Comparative and Historical Perspective: An International Handbook and Research Guide.* Westport, CT: Greenwood, pp. 217–240; Harkness, S., & Super, C.M. (1992). The developmental niche: A theoretical framework for analyzing the household production of health. *Social Science and Medicine, 38* (2), 217–226; Harkness, S., & Super, C.M. (1992). The cultural foundations of fathers' roles: Evidence from Kenya and the United States. In B.S. Hewlett (Ed.), *The Father's Role: Cultural and Evolutionary Perspectives.* New York: Aldine de Gruyter, pp. 191–211.

22 Draper, P., & Cashdan, E. (1988). Technological change and child behavior among the !Kung. *Ethnology, 27,* 339–365.

23 Edwards, C.P., & Whiting, B.B. (Eds.). (2004). *Ngecha: A Kenyan Village in a Time of Rapid Social Change.* Lincoln, NE: University of Nebraska Press.

24 Whiting, B.B., & Whiting, J.W.M. (1975). *The Children of Six Cultures: A Psychocultural Analysis.* Cambridge, MA: Harvard University Press.

25 Whiting, B.B., & Edwards, C.P. (1988). *Children of Different Worlds: The Formation of Social Behavior.* Cambridge, MA: Harvard University Press.

26 Super, C., & Harkness, S. (1986). The developmental niche: A conceptualization at the interface of child and culture. *International Journal of Behavioral Development, 9,* 545–569.

5 Culture, socio-economic status and educational outcomes

三歳定八十

Chinese saying: A child at 3 determines the adult at 80

The income that anyone earns is dependent on their education and capabilities. The link between educational performance and labour market outcomes is well documented,[1] and research has identified that at least some of the disadvantages of minority ethnic groups can be traced to their educational attainment.[2] This suggests a need to consider the education achievement of ethnic groups.

Variations in academic achievement between ethnic groups are well documented.[3] In the United States, African American and Hispanic children tend to score lower than white children in multiple areas, including reading and maths. These gaps appear at a young age. For example, Lee and Burkham (2002) noted that the average maths score of Hispanic and African American children at kindergarten entry was nearly 20% lower than white children.[4] Fryer and Levitt (2004) observed that this gap increased during the kindergarten year, from one-half to nearly three-quarters of a standard deviation.[5] The gaps continue to widen over time.[6]

Explanations for the poor academic achievement fall into three categories.[7] One explanation claims that cultures vary in the value they place upon achievement.[8] Put simply, some groups are not highly motivated towards achievement. These arguments build on Weber's Protestant ethic claiming that ethnic groups have cultural orientations which can assist or limit economic development.[9] For example, Rosen (1959) argued that high motivation for achievement can be found among Protestants, Greeks and Jews.[10] However, French Canadians, Southern Italians and blacks have lower vocational aspirations.

The second explanation emphasises the structural position of ethnic groups taking into account their time of arrival as migrants. This includes the skills they brought with them and the skills needed in their new economy.[11] With this in mind, it is noteworthy that many of the poorer-performing immigrant groups gain entry to their host country on the basis that they were employed in low-skilled areas. In the lower echelons of society, the children are exposed to poorer quality educational opportunities.

Some explanations fall in between these arguments.[12] Ogbu (1978) claimed that those who voluntarily migrated willingly searched for the opportunities that the new society provided, whereas involuntary minorities such as indigenous peoples and slaves, developed an opposition culture in resistance to mainstream society.[13] Ogbu argued that past experiences led African Americans to distrust the dominant society and they developed norms to distinguish themselves from whites. Their youth developed an oppositional identity to the dominant white culture. For example, black students would criticise each other if they acted white and those with good grades were accused of being 'brainiacs'.

A third and more popular explanation focuses on the effect that poverty has on educational outcomes. A large body of research reveals that poverty and low socio-economic status (SES) has a negative effect on child development, including cognitive, academic and socio-emotional functioning.[14]

Socio-economic status affects educational outcomes in a number of ways. First is resources. Children growing up in low-income families have fewer educational resources. Access to reading material is important for the development of literacy and this deficiency can continue throughout the school years. For example, Entwisle et al. (1997) found that children from low SES families lost ground over summer when schools were closed, whereas children from high SES backgrounds continued to make academic progress, thus illustrating the importance of home resources such as books, computers and trips.[15]

A second effect of poverty is on health and nutrition. Children living in poverty may have nutritional deficits which can affect their cognitive development and concentration.[16] They are likely to have weaker access to quality health care and suffer more from illness. Children living in poverty are exposed to more violence, family separations and household instability.[17]

Economic strain can cause parents to experience psychological stress which leads to ineffective parenting styles.[18] Vericker et al. (2010) found that more than half of low-income mothers have some form of depression, and 11% have severe depression.[19] Depressed and stressed mothers talk less with their children,[20] hence their children have slower vocabulary growth.[21]

Parenting practices differ in lower SES families. Hess and Holloway (1984) identified differences in the verbal interactions between mothers and children, expectations of parents for achievement, and discipline and control strategies.[22] There are also differences in the amount of emotional support and cognitive stimulation that children receive.[23]

Research has found a strong link between SES and parenting strategies. Bradley and Corwyn (2002) argued that parents with high socio-economic status engage in a number of practices linked to better intellectual and academic development in children.[24] These include reading to children, engaging in more speech with their children and using a richer vocabulary. The extent to which parents monitor their children also increases with socio-economic advantage.

One reason for this may be maternal education. Mothers in higher SES families are likely to have more years of formal schooling, and research suggests that maternal education is 'the component of SES most strongly related to child development outcomes'.[25]

The socio-economic mix of children's neighbourhoods is also related to schooling outcomes. Adolescents with affluent neighbours complete more years of school and are less likely to drop out than those who grow up in poorer neighbourhoods.[26] This appears to reflect the effect of neighbourhood socialisation which provides role models, social norms and resource availability.[27]

It has been argued that ethnic minorities suffer because of the quality of schools they attend. This is supported by a body of research which revealed that schools perpetuate disparities.[28] The explanation has merit given that, at school, the teacher replaces the parent as the principle educator, and the gap between races increases at school. However, even when schooling is of the same quality, students get uneven returns from the same education. This draws attention to the capabilities children possess when they enter school. If children enter school with low academic ability, they will not benefit from schooling as much as those who enter at higher levels. This 'accumulation of experiences' is responsible for a widening of the gap between the haves and have-nots.[29]

Potter and Morris (2017) found that accumulation of advantage and disadvantage is an important factor to consider when studying educational inequality.[30] They found that African American and Hispanic children accumulated fewer beneficial educational experiences compared with their white peers. However, accumulated experience did not explain all of the gap. indicating other factors were also important.

The parent's role is not eliminated once children start school. Many parents continue to play an active role supporting the child's education. For example, the academic success of Asian Americans has been linked to the expectations of the parents and the importance placed on learning in Asian American families.[31] Family values can also influence engagement in extra-curricular activities which also has been linked with superior academic performance.[32] Notably, research reveals that black and Hispanic students are likely to engage in less extra-curricular activity than white students.[33]

A final explanation for poor academic performance, not favoured by researchers for its racist implications, is that poor performing ethnic groups have lower intelligence due to genetics. Behavioural geneticists do not deny the importance of socio-economic status and home environment; however, given that these factors occur within biologically related families, there is a possibility that the low income and home environment is influenced by genetic factors.[34]

Developments in neuroscience make the racial explanation less plausible. The brain's potential is highly variable and capable of 'neuroplasticity'.[35] This refers to the brain's ability to re-wire and achieve enhanced potential. It means that new neural pathways can be made and strengthened so, even if there were genetic differences, it is unlikely that neural limits have been reached in any ethnic group.

Early experience, in particular, can modify the genetic architecture of neural circuits.[36] Neural pathways are built by daily activity and stimulus in the environment. So even if we accept a genetic explanation, the expression of those genes is strongly shaped by environmental conditions.[37] The home environment in particular can strongly influence a child's neural development. This suggests an explanation (and solution) for poor academic performance may lie in understanding the home environment and culture passed through parental behaviour.

Chinese educational success

One last explanation for poverty among ethnic minorities is discrimination. However, the problem with discrimination as an explanation is that some very distinctive ethnic groups are doing well, in particular Asians. Their distinctive difference to the white majority would make them prime targets for discrimination yet, they still do very well. Their success makes discrimination an unlikely explanation. More positively, if we can understand the reason for their success, it may help us understand and solve poverty in different ethnic groups.

Chinese students face similar barriers to other ethnic minorities at school. They are a visually distinctive ethnic minority which could expose them to discriminatory treatment. They have a strong respect for authority, and dislike being embarrassed which affects risk taking. They must learn in English, a second language, and are operating in a second culture and institutional environment. While these factors can be a barrier to learning, Chinese students overcome them. In fact, Chinese educational success is repeated in Western nations around the world. Chinese pupils consistently out-perform others.[38]

The Chinese economy has long held peculiarities that have generated very different behaviours in terms of education. China had a high population-to-resource base which meant that investment in human capital was necessary. It also increased competition which generated a strong work ethic. It was a literate society with a tradition of formal education, and that education was valued. Since the introduction of the Confucian education system, scholars have been placed at the top of China's social hierarchy, giving education high cultural value.

Another aspect of Chinese culture is the role of the family. It was the children's responsibility to look after their parents in their old age. This meant the parents did everything they could to encourage their children's education for, in so doing, they laid foundations of their income in their old age. These routines, behaviours and values infiltrated other parts of Asia and, to this day, Asian Americans are more likely to believe in the value of education for socio-mobility.[39]

Chinese parental patterns recently came to prominence with the release of *Battle Hymn of the Tiger Mother* in which the author claimed that Chinese parenting is superior to Western parenting.[40] Chua's book caused an uproar in the United States and the author was accused of being an abusive parent. The book revealed many differences between Western and Chinese parental styles. While Westerners laud their children as gifted or talented, Chinese emphasise hard work:

> the Chinese strategy produces a virtuous circle. Tenacious practice, practice, practice is crucial for excellence ... Once a child starts to excel at something—whether its math, piano, pitching or ballet—he or she gets praise, admiration

> and satisfaction. This builds confidence and makes the once not-fun activity fun. This in turn makes it easier for the parent to get the child to work even more.[41]

The book instigated scholarly discourse on the topic of tiger mums.[42] Much of the debate focused on Chua's perceived excessive control and heavy handedness. In the next section of this chapter, we examine parental styles that have influenced academic work on parenting. Chua's description fits that of an authoritarian style, a style not favoured in the West. With this in mind, we must remember that parenting is about more than academic success and includes a wide range of development activities.

Nevertheless, many aspects of Amy Chua's parenting are supported by research. For example, Chao (1994) studied the parental styles of immigrant Chinese mothers and found that their culture plays a critical role in shaping parental goals and how children are encouraged to bring honour to the family.[43] She noted that tighter control was consistent with their care and concern for their children. She used the term *guanjiao* to refer to that caring, monitoring, teaching and training. Chinese parents spend much longer mentoring their children than Westerners.

Chua's (2011) book describes the content of some of her mentoring. It went beyond reading to the children, and included mentoring of study techniques, for example the need to triple-check answers and verifying the meanings of new words. It also included subject content, and the level of analysis provided by Chua was striking.[44] To provide this level of mentoring, a parent must have some educational skills. Not surprisingly, Kao and Thompson (2003) state that parental education, together with family income, is probably the best indicator of academic outcomes.[45] In this regard, Asian American youth are extremely advantaged in terms of parental education levels.

By contrast, Pacific people living in New Zealand do not have the same educational expertise which suggests they will find it hard to provide the same level of mentoring. Not surprisingly, surveys of Pacific students reveal that a lack of parental understanding and support for school-related activities potentially inhibits their progress.[46] This education difference can reflect culturally induced behaviours and immigration selection criteria. Pacific people do not generally enter New Zealand under categories that require educational attainment. However, it also recognises the difficulty of behaviour acquisition when you 'do not know what you do not know'. If you have little knowledge of what is needed for educational success, it is hard to impart it to your children.

Chinese mothers imbue in their children the idea that effort generates success, not ability.[47] If children fail, they have not worked hard enough, and this generates behaviours that include long hours of work. This stands in sharp contrast to the Pacific students we will describe later, who contribute success to luck or brains. Other academics have confirmed this. Leung (1995) confirms the Chinese emphasis on effort as an explanation for achievement.[48] Chinese students gain a view of learning as a process of moral striving called *self-perfection*.[49]

Research conducted by Carol Dweck in the 1990s would support a strong emphasis on effort.[50] Dweck gave children a task to complete, after which they were told that they had performed well and achieved a high score (regardless of their actual score). Some of the children were then praised and told 'you must be smart at these problems', while others were told 'you must have worked hard at these problems'.

Dweck found that those who were praised for their effort tended to work harder the next time, showed more resilience and enjoyed the process and accomplishment more. The results indicated that encouraging the children to work hard provided better development outcomes than praising them for their abilities.

Chinese parents exercise strong control of extra-curricular activities, a behaviour which researchers have recognised as aiding academic development. Annette Lareau's book *Unequal Childhoods* revealed that middle-class people favoured 'purposeful cultivation' and organised their children's extra-curricular activities.[51] By contrast, poorer families favoured 'natural growth' with unstructured leisure time which did not contribute to learning skills or preparation for professional life.

Chinese parental behaviour is not without criticism and there is no one answer to how best to bring up children.[52] However, if a group is succeeding in an area where another is weak, it is worthwhile comparing their different behaviours. The Chinese face many of the same barriers that other ethnic groups face, but the Chinese make those barriers look insignificant. Why is it that people from one culture stop at what seems an unsurpassable wall but others step over it with ease? This suggests we need to take a closer examination of the role of culture.

Parenting for a modern economy

The importance of parenting for child development is a well-developed area of study, and in this section, we will introduce some of the elements that contemporary researchers have identified for effective parenting. One of the most influential researchers was Diana Baumrind who, in 1967, stressed that the style of parenting has an important influence on a child's development.[53] She identified three different parenting styles which have differing impacts on children's behaviour, well-being and subsequent adult adjustment. The three parenting styles are 1) authoritative, 2) authoritarian and 3) permissive parenting styles.

These styles vary in the level of control and warmth the child is given. Control relates to the level of supervision and discipline. Warmth reflects the extent that the child is integrated into the family and fosters the child's self-reliance, individuality and self-assertiveness. The three parental styles vary in their level of warmth and control. The relationship between parenting styles and warmth and control can be seen in Table 5.1.

Parents practising an *authoritarian* style are low on warmth and high on control. This style allowed for little individualism from the child with the parents shaping the child by setting standards and imposing punishment. This can lead the child to be withdrawn and show maladaptive behaviour later in life. Authoritarian

Table 5.1 Warmth, control and parental style

	High warmth	*Low warmth*
High control	Authoritative	Authoritarian
Low control	Permissive	Disengaged

parenting is the style practised by Chinese Tiger Mothers as described by Amy Chua. Hence, when her book was published, she was seen as advocating an inferior parental style. It might produce gifted scholars, but many developmental psychologists would argue that a more holistic parenting approach is needed. Nevertheless, academic success is important to create the human capital that contributes to wealth or poverty.

The second parenting style identified by Baumrind is *Permissive* parenting. Permissive parents are the opposite to Authoritarian parents. They are high on warmth but low on control. They use less discipline and are more compliant with the wishes of their children. However, this parental style can suffer from a lack of structure. Parents are highly responsive to their children but this can become indulgent with little in the way of boundaries. Children growing in such environments can have high self-esteem but low self-control. They may be vulnerable to drugs and alcohol, and have problems forming relationships.

The last parental style is labelled *Authoritative* parenting. It is high on both control and warmth. Children are disciplined but it is not done just by the use of power. Parents reason with their children to make them aware of the need to modify their behaviours. Parents provide strong sense of structure, but still allow some freedoms. Such children grow with a sense of responsibility, high self-esteem and independence.

In recent years, a fourth style of parenting has been identified, that is 'disengaged' parenting. The behaviour of disengaged parents is low in both warmth and control. It has been linked to many negative outcomes for children including impulsivity, behavioural and emotional problems, school dropout, substance abuse and delinquency. By contrast, the best social, cognitive and behavioural developmental outcomes for children are linked to authoritative parenting which embodies high levels of warmth and control.[54]

Today, there are many different dimensions and typologies for assessing parental behaviour but warmth and control remain two commonly used elements. In fact, control has been broken down further in to psychological control, behavioural control and monitoring.[55] *Psychological control* refers to parental strategies to manage the child's emotional or psychological processes. It may involve withdrawing love, inducing guilt and shame. A high use of these strategies can have a negative impact on a child's self-esteem and maturity.[56] By contrast, *behavioural control* refers to parental communication and enforcement of rules and restrictions to manage the child's behaviour. Insufficient behavioural control can result in behavioural problems in youth.

Parental monitoring refers to the extent that parents monitor their child's whereabouts, structure the child home, school and community engagements and keep track of the child's behaviour. It also includes the extent to which a parent has knowledge on the child's whereabouts, activities and friends. High levels of parental monitoring are associated with positive child outcomes. Poor parental monitoring, by contrast is directly linked with child behavioural problems and poor school achievement.[57]

Another important element in parenting is *communication*. The quality of parent–child communication has been found to impact on child development.[58] Effective and high-quality communication increases feelings of security and attachment, with consequent improvement in the quality of the parent–child relationship.[59] The quality of communication determines the effectiveness of discipline and the establishment of rules, expectations and consequences of behaviour.

Another relevant line of work is that of attachment theory. This theory stresses the importance of a secure attachment bond between a baby and its care-giver. According to this theory, the early relationship serves as a model that the child transposes onto other relationships in life. Hence, a secure stable attachment facilitates greater success in social relationships. Children grow to be more empathetic and are better at initiating and facilitating relationships. The child benefits from higher self-esteem with good levels of mental health and personal adjustment.[60]

Secure attachments during childhood have also been found to be important for the child's moral development. This is linked with the child's internalisation levels and the existence of non-fearful/anxious temperaments.[61] Secure attachment has also been linked to the development of moral reasoning,[62] that is, how they think about and accept moral behaviour.

Moral development has also been linked to democratic styles of parenting in which pro-social behaviour, such as helping and sharing, is positively reinforced, while selfish behaviour is inhibited.[63] Under democratic parenting, solving problems is done through rational explanation. This is more effective than power and

Table 5.2 Parental constructs

Warmth – is defined by expressions of physical and emotional support and love.

Behavioural control – consists of strategies to manage children's behavioural functioning through the use of rules, regulations and expectations and the consistent enforcement of these rules and regulations.

Psychological control – includes strategies to manage children's emotional or psychological processes and the use of maternal psychological and emotional processes to manage behaviour (e.g., shaming, guilt, love withdrawal).

Monitoring – represents parental supervision and knowledge of the children's whereabouts, activities and friends.

Communication – refers to the frequency of discussions and degree of positive and negative exchanges during discussions.

Parental self efficacy – is defined as a parent's rating of perceived ability to be a competent parent.

Source: Le et al. (2008).

threat-based techniques as the latter are more likely to arouse negative emotions such as rage and hostility.[64]

In later chapters of this book, we will expand on parental behaviours, with a focus on academic socialisation as this has important implications for a child's educational outcomes and long-term earning potential.

Notes

1 Kao, G., & Thompson, J. (2003). Racial and ethnic stratification in educational achievement and attainment. *Annual Review of Sociology*, 29, 417–442.
2 Jencks, C. (1972). *Inequality: A Reassessment of the Effect of Family and Schooling in America*. New York: Basic Books; Rivera-Batiz (2007).
3 Condron, D.J. (2009). Social class, school and non-school environments, and black/white inequalities in children's learning. *American Sociological Review*, 74, 683–708; Downey, D.B., von Hippel, P.T., & Broh, B.A. (2004). Are school the great equalizer? Cognitive Inequality during the summer months and the school year. *American Sociological Review*, 69, 613–35.
4 Lee, V.E., & Burkham, D.T. (2002). *Inequality at the Starting Gate: Social Background Differences in Achievement as Children Begin School*. Washington, DC: Economic Policy Institute.
5 Fryer, R.G., & Levitt, S.D. (2004). Understanding the black–white test score gap in the first two years of school. *The Review of Economics and Statistics*, 86, 447–64.
6 Potter, D., & Morris, D.S. (2017). Family and schooling experiences in racial/ethnic academic achievement gaps: A cumulative perspective. *Sociological Perspectives, 60*(1), 132–167.
7 Kao & Thompson (2003).
8 McClelland, D.C., Atkinson, J.W., Clark, R.A., & Lowell, E.L. (1953). *The Achievement Motive*. New York: Appleton-Century-Crofts.
9 Harrison, L.E. (1985). *Underdevelopment is a State of Mind: The Latin American Case*. Lanham, MD: University Press of America; Harrison, L.E., & Huntington, S. (Eds.). (2000). *Culture Matters: How Values Shape Human Progress*. New York: Basic Books.
10 Rosen, B.C. (1959). Race, ethnicity, and the achievement syndrome. *American Sociological Review, 24*, 47–60.
11 Steinberg, L. (1996). *Beyond the Classroom: Why School Reform Has Failed and What Parents Need to Do*. New York: Simon & Schuster; Lieberson S. (1980). *A Piece of Pie: Black and White Immigrants since 1880*. Berkeley: University of California Press.
12 Kao & Thompson (2003).
13 Ogbu, J.U. (1978). *Minority Education and Caste: The American System in Cross-cultural Perspective*. New York: Academic Press.
14 Huston, A., McLoyd, V.C., & García Coll, C. (1994). Children and poverty: Issues in contemporary research. *Child Development, 65*, 275–282.
15 Entwisle, D., Alexander, K., & Olson, L. (1997). *Children, Schools, and Inequality*. Boulder, CO: Westview Press.
16 Ermisch, J. (2008). Origins of social immobility and inequality: Parenting and early child development. *National Institute Economic Review*, 205(1), 62–71.
17 Evans, G.W. (2004). The environment of childhood poverty. *American Psychologist*, 59, 77–92.
18 Blair, C., & Raver, C.C. (2012). Child development in the context of adversity: Experiential canalization of brain and behavior. *American Psychologist*, 67, 309–18; Guo, G., & Harris, K.M. (2000). The mechanisms mediating the effects of poverty on children's intellectual development. *Demography*, 37(4), 431–447.

19 Vericker, T., Macomber, J., & Golden, O.A. (2010). *Infants of Depressed Mothers Living in Poverty: Opportunities to Identify and Serve*. Report. Washington, DC: Urban Inst.
20 Lovejoy, M.C., Graczyk, P.A., O'Hare, E., & Newman, G. (2000). Maternal depression and parenting behavior: A meta-analytic review. *Clinical Psychology Review*, 20, 561–592.
21 Pan, B.A., Rowe, M.L., Singer, J.D., & Snow, C.E. (2005). Maternal correlates of growth in toddler vocabulary production in low-income families. *Child Development*, 76, 763–782.
22 Hess, R., & Holloway, S. (1984). Family and school as educational institutions. In R. D. Parke (Ed.), *Review of Child Development Research*, Vol. 7. Chicago: University of Chicago Press, pp. 179–222.
23 Korenman, S., Miller, J., & Sjaastad, J. (1995). Long-term poverty and child development in the United States: Results from the NLSY. *Children and Youth Services Review*, 17, 127–155.
24 Bradley, R.H., & Corwyn, R.F. (2002). Socioeconomic status and child development. *Annual Review Psychology*, 53, 371–399.
25 Hoff, E., Laursen, B., & Bridges, K. (2002). Measurement and model building in studying the influence of socioeconomic status on child development. In Lewis, M. and Mayes, L. (Eds), *A Developmental Environmental Measurement Handbook*, pp. 590–606. New York: Cambridge University Press; Magnuson, K.A., Sexton, H.R., Davis-Kean, P.E., & Huston, A.C. (2009). Increases in maternal education and young children's language skills. *Merrill-Palmer Quarterly*, 55, 319–50.
26 Brooks-Gunn, J., Duncan, G., Klebanov, P., & Sealand, N. (1993). Do neighborhoods influence child and adolescent development? *American Journal of Sociology, 99*, 353–395. Corcoran et al. (1992); Datcher, L. (1982). Effects of community and family background on achievement. *Review of Economics and Statistics*, 64, 32–41; Duncan, G. (1994). Families and neighbors as sources of disadvantage in the schooling decisions of White and Black adolescents. *American Journal of Education*, 103, 20–53.
27 Brooks-Gunn, Duncan et al. (1993); Duncan (1994).
28 Halpern-Manner, A., Warren, J.R., & Brand J.E. (2009). Dynamic measures of primary and secondary school characteristics: Implications for school effects research. *Social Science Research*, 38, 397–411.
29 DiPrete, T.A., & Eirich, G.M. (2006). Cumulative advantage as a mechanism for inequality: A review of theoretical and empirical developments. *Annual Review of Sociology*, 32, 271–297.
30 Potter & Morris (2017).
31 Kao & Thompson (2003); Pomerantz, E.M., Ng, F.F.-Y., & Wang, Q. (2008). Culture, parenting, and motivation: The case of East Asia and the United States. *Social Psychological Perspective*, 15, 209–240; Steinberg (1996).
32 Covay, E., & Carbonaro, W. (2010). After the bell: Participation in extracurricular activities, classroom behavior, and academic achievement. *Sociology of Education*, 83, 20–45; Morris, D. (2015). Actively closing the gap? Social class, organized activities, and academic achievement in high school. *Youth and Society*, 47, 267–290.
33 Morris (2015).
34 Rowe, D., & Rodgers, J. (1997). Poverty and behavior: Are environmental measures nature and nurture? *Developmental Review*, 17, 358–375; Scarr, S. (1993). Biological and cultural diversity: The legacy of Darwin for development. *Child Development*, 64, 1333–1353.
35 Pascual-Leone, A., Amedi, A., Fregni, F., & Merabet, L.B. (2005). The plastic human brain cortex. *Annual Review of Neuroscience, 28*, 377–401.
36 Knudsen, E.I. (2004). Sensitive periods in the development of the brain and behavior. *Journal of Cognitive Neuroscience*, October, *16*, 1412–1425.

37 Caspi, A., McClay, J., Moffitt, T.E., Mill, J., Martin, J., Craig, I.W., Taylor, A., & Poulton, R. (2002). Role of genotype in the cycle of violence in maltreated children. *Science, 297*, 851–854.

38 Centre for Ethnicity and Racism Studies. (2006). *Chinese Pupils' Experiences within British and American Educational Contexts.* Downloaded from: http://www.sociology.leeds.ac.uk/; Archer, L., & Francis, B. (2007). *Understanding Minority Ethnic Achievement: Race, Gender, Class and 'Success'.* London: Routledge.

39 Kao, G., & Thompson, J.S. (2003). Racial and ethnic stratification in educational achievement and attainment. *Annual Review of Sociology*, 29, 417–442.

40 Chua, A. (2011). *Battle Hymn of the Tiger Mother.* London: Bloomsbury.

41 Ibid., p. 29.

42 Kim, S.Y. (2013). Defining tiger parenting in Chinese Americans. *Human Development, 56*, 217–222.

43 Chao, R.K. (1994). Beyond parental control and authoritarian parenting style: Understanding Chinese parenting through the cultural notion of training. *Child Development*, 65, 1111–1119.

44 Chua (2011).

45 Kao & Thompson (2003).

46 Fletcher, J., Parkhill, F., Fa'afoi, A., & O'Regan, B. (2009). Pasifika students: Teachers and parents voice their perceptions of what provides supports and barriers to Pasifika students' achievement in literacy and learning. *Teaching and Teacher Education, 25*, 24–33; Fletcher, J., Parkhill, F., Taleni, T., & Fa'afoi, A. (2006). Pasifika students' perceptions of barriers and support to reading and writing achievement in New Zealand schools. *New Zealand Journal of Educational Studies*, 41, 163–182.

47 Kohler, M., Aldridge, J., Christensen, L.M., & Kilgo, J. (2012). Issues in education: Tiger moms: Five questions that need to be answered. *Childhood Education, 88*, 52–53; Kim, S. Y., & Wong, V.Y. (2002). Assessing Asian and Asian American parenting: A review of the literature. In K. Kurasaki, S. Okazaki & S. Sue (Eds.), *Asian American Mental Health: Assessment Theories and Methods*, New York: Kluwer, pp.185–201; Li, J. (2012). *Cultural Foundations of Learning: East and West.* New York: Cambridge University Press.

48 Leung, K. (2010). Beliefs in Chinese culture. In M.H. Bond (Ed.), *The Oxford Handbook of Chinese Psychology.* Oxford: Oxford Library of Psychology, pp. 221–240.

49 Li, J. (2002). A cultural model of learning: Chinese 'heart and mind for wanting to learn'. *Journal of Cross-Cultural Psychology, 33*(3), 248–269.

50 Mueller, C.M., & Dweck, C.S. (1998). Praise for intelligence can undermine children's motivation and performance. *Journal of Personality and Social Psychology, 75*(1), 33–52; Dweck, C. (2012). *Mindset: How You Can Fulfil Your Potential.* London: Constable & Robinson.

51 Lareau, A. (2003). *Unequal Childhoods: Class, Race, and Family Life.* Berkeley: University of California Press.

52 Suissa, J. (2013). Tiger mothers and praise junkies: Children, praise and the reactive attitudes. *Journal of Philosophy of Education, 47*, 1–19.

53 Baumrind, D. (1967). Child care practices anteceding three patterns of preschool behavior. *Genetic Psychology Monographs*, 75(1), 43–88.

54 Wake, M., Nicholson, J.M., Hardy, P., & Smith, K. (2007). Preschooler obesity and parenting styles of mothers and fathers: Australian national population study. *Pediatrics, 120*(6), e1520–e1527; Baumrind, D. (1991). The influence of parenting style on adolescent competence and substance use. *The Journal of Early Adolescence, 11*(1), 56–95.

55 Barber, B.K., Stolz, H.E., & Olsen, J.A. (2005). Parental support, psychological control, and behavioral control: Assessing relevance across time, culture, and method. *Monographs of the Society for Research in Child Development, 70*(4), 1–137.

56 Le, H.N., Ceballo, R., Chao, R., Hill, N.E., Murry, V.M., & Pinderhughes, E.E. (2008). Excavating culture: Disentangling ethnic differences from contextual influences in parenting. *Applied Development Science, 12*(4), 163–175.

57 Spera, C. (2005). A review of the relationship among parenting practices, parenting styles, and adolescent school achievement. *Educational Psychology Review*, 17, 125–146.
58 Murry, V., Brody, G.H., McNair, L.D., Luo, Z., Gibbons, F.X., Gerrard, M., & Wills, T.A. (2005). Parental involvement promotes rural African American youths' self-pride and sexual self-concepts. *Journal of Marriage and the Family, 67*, 627–642.
59 Le et al. (2008).
60 Sroufe, L.A. (2002). From infant attachment to promotion of adolescent autonomy: Prospective, longitudinal data on the role of parents in development. In J.G. Borkowsky, S. Landesman Ramey, & M. Bristol-Power (Eds.), *Parenting and the Child's World: Influences on Academic, Intellectual, and Social-emotional Development.* Mahwah, NJ: LEA Publishers, pp. 187–202.
61 Kochanska, G. (1995). Children's temperament, mother's discipline, and security of attachment: Multiple pathways to emerging internalization. *Children Development, 66*, 597–615.
62 Van Ijzendoorn, M.H., & Zwart-Woudstra, G. (1995). Adolescents' attachment representations and moral reasoning. *The Journal of Genetic Psychology, 156*, 359–372.
63 Holden, G.W. (1997). *Parents and the Dynamics of Child Rearing.* Oxford: Westview Press.
64 Freijo, E.B.A. (2005) *Family Context and Psychological Development in Early Childhood: Educational Implications.* Downloaded from http://www.haezi.org/uploads/files/ultimaspublicaciones/MarylandFormat1.Language.July03.pdf.

6 Neuroplasticity and ethnotheories

> Different types of brain produce different culture and different types of culture produce different brains ...
>
> Biologist Robert Sapolsky[1]

What is neuroplasticity?

To understand how parenting affects human potential, it is necessary to understand the concept of neuroplasticity and how different cultures lead to different developmental outcomes. Neuroplasticity refers to how neural pathways in the brain are changed through experience. The idea that the structure of our brains can change may come as a surprise to many people, but it is an ongoing process that continues throughout our lifetime as we learn new things or memorise new information.

The working units of the brain are the neurons. They are specialised cells that transmit information to other nerve cells or other parts of the body. The brain comprises billions of connections between neurons located in different parts of the brain. These connections facilitate communication within the brain and activate specialised areas of activity. The brain's structure is built up over time as neural connections are formed. Hence, the brain develops over time, going through a number of stages that begin before birth and continue into adulthood.[2]

Neurons comprise axons which send information out and dendrites which receive information. The link between one neuron's axon and another neuron's dendrite is called a synaptic connection. The simplest neural connections are formed while the child is still in the womb. At the time of birth each neuron in the cerebral cortex has approximately 2,500 synapses.[3] However, the number of synapses increases dramatically in the first years of life.

After birth, the brains of babies are flooded with stimulation. This information is processed in the brain which grows rapidly. More neural connections are formed and, by the age of 2 or 3 years, an infant will have approximately 15,000 synapses per neuron.[4]

Of note, the number of synaptic connections in infants of this age is twice that of the average adult brain. That is because as we age, old and disused connections are deleted in a process called synaptic pruning. Strong connections that have been strengthened through use will not be deleted. Hence, we can see how experience shapes brain structure. It shapes what neural connections are formed and maintained.

From this description, we can see the problem with James Watson's explanation that genetics determines intelligence differences between racial groups. Genetics is a factor in the brain's structure as it provides the initial blueprint on which neuroplasticity acts. However, neuroplasticity itself is formed by interaction with the environment. It is our experiences and the actions that we engage in that determine which connections are formed and maintained. As Kolb and Gibb (2011: 65) note:

> The development of the brain reflects more than the simple unfolding of a genetic blueprint but rather reflects a complex dance of genetic and experiential factors that shape the emerging brain. Understanding the dance provides insight into both normal and abnormal development.[5]

With more than 100,000 trillion synapses in the cerebral cortex, the number of synapse formations is well above the genetic blueprint laid down in our DNA.[6] Genes may provide a blueprint, but the expression of those genes is altered and shaped by specific experience which is reflected in changes in the nervous system. This, in turn, has implications for development outcomes as the child grows. However, variations in personal experiences can result in dramatic differences in cerebral circuitry.[7]

The first years of life are the time when most neural connections are being established and refined. Hence, an infant's environment and interactions play an important role in determining brain architecture. It is a period when the brain is particularly sensitive to the stimulus it receives. This period of sensitivity is the same time that the foundations for the child's future social skills and cognitive linguistic capacities emerge, as well as their emotional and physical health. These foundations have consequences for success in school, the workplace and the larger community.[8] Therefore, what happens in early childhood can have implications for development and outcomes throughout a person's life.

The process of neuroplasticity continues as we age. In fact, the brain never stops changing, but the rate of change does slow. Hence children find it easier to learn foreign languages than adults. Similarly, a child that has suffered brain damage will enjoy faster repair than an adult.

Of course, this means that some experiences can have a negative impact. Stress weakens the brains architecture. Diet too can have an influence. Hence, many studies will logically note that if low-income families have more stress and poorer diets, this will affect brain development. However, stress by itself is not a problem. In fact, it is a healthy part of development. A problem only exists when it prolonged.[9] Of course, poor families are not the only ones to eat badly or experience stress, and not all poor families suffer from this. Nevertheless, as this suggests, not all plasticity is favourable to development. One need only note how drugs can change neural pathways and lead to addiction.

A word that regularly appears among the academic literature is 'enrichment'; that is, providing an enriched environment that favours brain development. This is not restricted to humans. Neuroscientists have found that placing an animal in a complex environment in which animals can interact with changing sensory and social stimulus results in a large range of neural changes including increased neuron size, synapses per neuron, cortical thickness, dendritic branching, glial numbers and complexity and overall brain size.[10] Kolb and Gibbs stress:

> The magnitude of these changes should not be underestimated.[11]

For example, a study which housed young rats in enriched environments resulted in increases in brain weight of between 7% and 10%, yet the rats were only in this environment for 60 days.[12] The authors estimate an increase in synapses in the cortex of about 20%. They describe the changes in brain structure resulting from an enriched environment as 'extraordinary'.

There are clear lessons emerging from the work of neuroscientists that an enriched environment can produce long-lasting changes in the brain. The most important time for enrichment is in the earliest years when connection formation is at its highest. Experiences affect the brain differently depending on the age of the person (and animal) and the impact can be complex. Neuroscientists Bryan Kolb and Robbin Gibb conclude

> these early experiences have a powerful effect on brain organization both during development and in adulthood.[13]

And the prime source of enrichment in these early years is the people who shape the family environment and have the most interaction with the infant; that is the parents:

> there is little doubt that the parent-child relationships are critical and that they play a key role in brain development. Differences in the pattern of early maternal-infant interactions can initiate long-term developmental effects that persist into adulthood.[14]

As we are about to read, this work of the neuroscientists mirrors findings from developmental psychologists.

Parenting ethnotheories

There is a large area of agreement between the work of the neuroscientists and developmental psychologists. For example, Leyendecker et al. (2011) state:

> The relationship between children's early child-rearing environment and their cognitive development is well established and is considered to be an important predictor for later school achievement … Parents who provide a stimulating

> environment for their children and engage in various forms of dyadic interaction such as playing and joint book reading are likely to support their children's emerging cognitive skills.[15]

The authors back this statement with a long list of research citations.[16] The education that children receive in their early years is guided by culturally specific convictions about what is appropriate for children to learn and develop during their first years of life.[17]

Studies of parenting in the West have identified a number of parental behaviours that are likely to enhance cognitive development in children, as one would expect from the above descriptions. The first is to provide an enriched environment with books and toys and experiences such as visiting shops and libraries.[18] Some of these activities require financial resources and suggest that poverty might hinder development outcomes.

The importance of resources has particular emphasis for some immigrants who have fewer resources, and this shortage can contribute to an inter-generational poverty trap. Unsurprisingly, a body of research links academic performance of children to poverty. The situation for immigrants is made worse by language barriers which inhibits their options to get support. Cultural barriers may also exist. Bourdieu's (1977) theory of social reproduction argues that a child's abilities are strongly influenced by cultural capital, and these cannot be improved unless the child has some familiarity with the dominant culture.[19]

However, a second feature is not resource dependent; that is, the quality and quantity of interactions a child has with its parents. The benefit of high-quality parent–child interaction does not just benefit cognitive development but also their language and socio-emotional capabilities.[20] Such interactions may include joint activities such as reading, but most important is the time spent by parents being involved in their children's lives.

In recent years, developmental psychologists have shown interest in ethnotheories and behaviours of parents in different cultures. Parenting ethnotheories can be described as

> ideas about adequate parental care and its developmental consequences, that are shared within cultural groups and reflect wider cultural models … These beliefs inform specific parenting behaviors, which shape developmental pathways of infants and children.[21]

These studies have revealed significant differences in the beliefs and practices of parents in different cultures. Parents all over the world make a substantial investment into their children and maintain specific beliefs about their care and handling.[22] These beliefs or ethnotheories are based on their societies' conceptions on the nature of children, parenting and development, and how best to nurture their capabilities for their respective environments.[23] These parental ethnotheories can be seen in the development goals that parents hold for their children.[24] There will, of course, be variations within cultures,[25] but members of cultural communities commonly share realities as to the importance of domains of life, developmental goals and the parenting styles relevant for the different stages of a child's development.[26]

There are notable differences between Western urban middle-class parents and parents in Africa and, as expected from the previous chapters, there is a big difference in the extent that parents stimulate motor and cognitive skills.

In sub-Saharan Africa, a large number of studies of a variety of ethnic groups show the high importance of motor stimulation together with the practice of caregivers to be in close contact with their infants. Ethnic groups studied include the Wolof,[27] the Gusii,[28] the Bambora,[29] Kipsigis and Kung San,[30] and the Nso.[31] These ethnic groups are all traditional rural communities based on a subsistence economy. They have low levels of formal education and their social values have an emphasis on hierarchal relatedness, that is cooperation is based on the roles they fill in society.

Parents in these societies see motor stimulation as a major dimension of parenting.[32] It is linked to the child's health, safety, mobility and ability of the child to participate early in the subsistence economy. Caregivers encourage the development of motor skills through 'motor stimulation', that is, through 'motor, vestibular and kinesthetic movements and exercises on the infant's body'.[33] Examples of such parental practices 'include rocking or swinging the infant, lifting him/her up and down, making him/her lie on its belly, sit, or stand'.[34]

By contrast, practices of motor stimulation are rarely stressed in Western urban middle-class families. Westerners believe that motor skills need time to develop and depends on each child's individual pace. There is also less emphasis on relatedness, and more of an emphasis on uniqueness and separateness from others.

In Germany, young infants are normally cared for by their mothers who usually take a year's maternity leave. The children spend most of their time in the presence of their mothers who orient their development to the external world around them. Sources of information to guide their practice can come from paediatricians, books and magazines.[35]

German parents place great value on interpersonal independence and cognitive competence. These development goals are reflected in German parental practice. The child is encouraged to explore and be creative to become unique agencies. This culture of independence and autonomy begins at a young age. Infants do not sleep with their parents, but sleep alone and there is reduced body contact. These practices reflect a society with high levels of formal education and economic prosperity, and a cultural model of psychological autonomy.

In encouraging autonomy, the child is also expected to develop a high degree of self-regulation (self-control). Cognitive development is also stressed and is supported with high levels of language input and face-to-face interaction between mother and child.[36] Of note, given the earlier discussion on Protestantism, northern Germany places a particularly strong emphasis on developing an independent parent–child relationship[37] (Northern Germany has traditionally been Protestant compared to Catholic southern Germany).

By contrast, the Nso community of West Africa do not show the same concern for independence and autonomy. As opposed to being self-regulated, there is an emphasis on relationships. Socialisation patterns are devoted to establishing harmonious and hierarchal relations between family members and the wider village.[38] Children are expected to be obedient and accept the authority of their parents. Infants do not sleep alone, but sleep with their mother and other siblings. During the day, the child is in close physical contact with their caregivers, being carried for almost the whole day.

Like other sub-Saharan African communities, the Nso place an emphasis on motor-skill development with the goal of developing muscle strength. This is done through a range of muscle stimulation practices. Parents have milestones for motor-skill development as rapid development enhances their ability to contribute to the families' subsistence and performance of chores.[39]

An interesting study contrasting women from northern Germany and those of the Nso was performed by Keller, Völker and Yovsi.[40] As the discussion above would suggest, they expected Nso women to focus on body stimulation, body contact and primary care. In contrast, they expected German women to focus on object stimulation, face-to-face exchange and to be sensitive towards positive infant signals.

To measure this, groups of German and Nso women were shown 20 videotapes of parenting behaviours from the two countries, after which the mothers could comment on the behaviours they observed. First, they watched videotapes of their own culture and in the second session, they watched videos from the foreign culture. After each tape the mothers stated what they thought was good or bad in the parent–child interaction and why they thought that way. Their answers were revealing.

As expected, there were significant differences in what the parents considered important. When assessing the quality of parenting, the Nso women referred more to primary care, body contact and body stimulation than the German groups. The researchers called these the three columns on which Nso parenting seemed to rest. In contrast, the German groups focus was on face-to-face contact, focus of attention, and sensitivity to negative signals.

In reference to primary care, the Nso women were very conscious of the health and hygiene of their infants which might possibly reflect that they came from a society with higher infant mortality rates. This could be seen in the Nso comments of the German's apparent lack of concern for hygiene and primary care. For example, one comment noted:

> the German mother is wiping the child's mouth with the hand instead of using a cloth.

The Nso concerns with German primary care was also seen in the reduced level of breast-feeding. A comment was:

> When the child is crying, the Germans just try to soothe it in a very funny way—without breastfeeding.

To the Nso, the Germans were deficient in their body contact. However, the Germans represented an individualistic culture which sought to develop a sense of independence and autonomy in their children. This did not sit comfortably with the Nso who thought there was a lack of physical and emotional closeness. The Nso women even began to suspect that German laws may forbid mothers to hold babies on their body:

> They handle them as if they are not their babies, as if it belongs to somebody else or as if they are a babysitter.

They also noted a lack of body stimulation. One particular comment captured the different emphasis on motor skills:

> Lifting the child up and down is not done there, and can lead to a retardation in the child's motor skills.

By contrast, the German women thought the practice of body stimulation was strange and expressed comments like 'They should not shake a small baby like this.' However, they certainly noticed the accelerated development in the Nso children. In fact, the German mothers unanimously doubted that the stated age of the child was accurate. They did not expect 3-month old children to show such development.

The Nso women were impressed by the German focus on language input, and their comments suggest they understand the link between this and the development of cognitive skills: 'The Germans are good in that they talk to their infants and that can enable their infants to learn language faster and to a better degree than Nso children', since 'for them, they believe every child is supposed to be intelligent.'

The Nso women recognised that talking to the babies was good as 'talking is necessary for language development' and language input increases children's language skills. From 'talking a child can learn pronouncing words and learn about things'. However, they saw it as an optional parenting strategy compared to the three important behaviours they stressed. It was a nice to have but its 'absence is never regretted'. In a modern knowledge-based economy, language abilities have much importance, but they do not have the same importance in Western Africa. Hence, they do not feature high in parenting strategies.

Another interesting study was conducted by Carra, Lavelli and Keller (2014) who examined 20 Italian and 20 West African immigrant mothers and their children. This study revealed more differing practices and the cultural knowledge that had been built behind it.[41] It is not just a case of developing motor skills, but how it was done. For example, West African mothers were aware that some motor-stimulation practices could scare the baby.

> when the mother performs holding movements for the first time, the infant is afraid, he may cry, but when "you continue lifting the baby up for many times, you teach her to not be afraid, to be strong and courageous" (IM4). Another mother said: "stretching the legs, the hands, and everything of the

> body makes the baby physically strong" (IM16). Therefore, they also clarified that the baby becomes used to be moved in this way, and "when she stops crying after the jumping, it means that she has overcome the fear" (IM13).[42]

In jumping games, the West African mothers stressed the importance of smiling to the baby because

> through the mother's smile "The baby knows that there is someone who loves her, she realizes that this is a way to be happy, and she begins to love" (IM4). At the same time, these mothers stated that during this interaction game they recognize the infant's positive emotions, such as happiness and enjoyment: "My baby enjoys and laughs very much, she feels to be like in the clouds, in the sky" (IM2). "He feels, he has the good sensation to be free in the empty space, but always sure to be held in my hands" (IM16).[43]

Practices are often accompanied with singing or rhythmic talking. Rhythm appears to be a salient dimension of West African parenting with repetitive communication and tactile stimulation. As these descriptions suggest, the motor stimulation is not just a process of capability development, but an act of mutual pleasure for the mother and infant.

Notably, the researchers found that some aspects of Western parenting were being adopted by the immigrant mothers, a reflection of the changing life context. Nevertheless, the emphasis on motor skills showed the durability and persistence of patterns brought from their original culture.

Other research has focused on the difference between German and Turkish parenting, noting the significant differences in their children's cognitive skills.[44] The differences in cognitive scores between German and Turkish children exist before children start school.[45] However, as with all populations, a proviso must be made in that substantial differences can occur within each nationality, reflecting parental education and, in the case of Turkish people, whether the family had rural or urban origins. Socio-economic disadvantage explains some of the disadvantage in Turkish achievement. Nevertheless, when research controls for socio-economic background, the inequality remains.[46]

Beidinger (2010) found that for children aged 3 to 4 years, the cognitive scores of Turkish children are about half a standard deviation worse than German children.[47] These differences rise as the children grow older. This is consistent with other studies which show that early differences increase over time. Immigrant children begin their education with significant disadvantages which lead to ongoing inequalities throughout their education. This could be expected to then be reflected in the job market and incomes.

Consistent with this, a number of important differences have been observed that affect how enriched the home environment is. Turkish parents are less likely to engage in parent–child play, as play to them is considered a child's activity conducted between children.[48] They are also less likely to read to their children or be involved in other ways.

An interesting finding from Citlak et al. (2010) was that Turkish parents living in Germany expected the school to be responsible for their child's formal education.[49] They did not see it as their role to provide the type of education given at schools. By contrast, German parents were aware that they had a responsibility in this area, especially the more educated parents. Notably, more educated Turkish parents were likely to have children with higher cognitive scores.

Of note is that differences in the home environment also led to inequalities within the German population studied. Once again, this highlights the importance of the home environment over genetics, hence Beidinger concludes:

> policy makers, educators and parents should emphasise the importance of joint parent–child activities as a means of reducing ethnic inequality.[50]

Beidinger does not claim that this is the only factor influencing outcomes and suggests other areas of research. Nevertheless, the message for policy-makers is becoming clear. There is a need to address early cognitive and academic inequalities.

Leyendecker et al. (2011) also studied German and Turkish parental practices.[51] They did this through a number of methods, including interviews and time budget diaries which recorded their activities, as well as tests on the children. Their study confirmed that Turkish immigrant children were less likely to be engaged in parent–child book-reading or other dyadic interaction. This is notable as these were positively related to children's cognitive performance. Other factors affecting cognitive performance of children are a stimulating home literacy environment, parental involvement, frequent visits of joint programmes for parents and children. Cognitive development is also negatively linked to rigid discipline practices. This is consistent with early research which noted that immigrant parents are likely to be less involved with their children and provide a less supportive environment for development. They also spend less time together.[52]

Notably, the effects of a stimulating home environment have been found to be more important than socio-economic origin.[53] An interesting aspect of Leyendecker et al.'s study, was that while the families' financial situation was important for Germans, it was not so for Turkish families. The Turkish mothers were not of low socio-economic status and were well above average with about ten years' education. What was most important for the cognitive scores of Turkish children was the extent that their parents provided a stimulating environment with an emphasis on positive interaction.

Whereas the studies cited above focused on parental behaviours, some studies focus on the development goals of parents. Moscardino, Bertelli and Altoè (2011) contrasted Italian and Romanian mothers and found that the Italians referred significantly more often to the autonomous and cognitive abilities of the child.[54] They emphasised self-fulfilment.

Self-fulfilment is not the goal of Africans. For example, Nigerian immigrant mothers living in Italy focus on 'a way of life that is respectful of other people and in accordance with their religious faith'.[55] As a whole, the immigrant groups tended to focus more on endorsing hierarchal relations rather than psychological autonomy found in the West.

Another study by Lavelli, Döge and Bighin (2016) examined the differences in development goals of four migrant groups to Italy and the perceptions of Italian preschool teachers.[56] The main goals expressed in the Italian curriculum for preschool education are development of children's identity, autonomy and personal competencies.[57] These goals are consistent with other urban Western societies characterised by a high proportion of middle-class families with high levels of formal education. In these societies, the focus of early child care is on the development of the child's individuality and cognitive achievement,[58] goals sometimes encompassed in the phrase 'psychological autonomy'. The societies from which migrants come may not share these goals.

Preschool teachers often find that children from different cultural backgrounds bring divergent behaviours (and languages) that make their job more demanding.[59] Lavelli, Döge and Bighin (2016) argue that the difficulties experienced integrating migrant children at host nation educational institutions may be due to discrepancies between what is expected at those institutions and the behaviours expected at home.[60]

Lavelli, Döge and Bighin (2016) studied the contrasting views of migrant mothers and those of preschool teachers.[61] They studied four migrant groups in Verona, Italy to discover the socialisation goals of mothers from Romania, Morocco, Nigeria and Sri Lanka. 'Respect for adults', 'religious practice' and 'sense of family's original culture' were all ranked highly. Sri Lankan mothers put an equal emphasis on social integration. The goal of 'respect for adults' was the highest for all migrant groups except the Moroccans who put the emphasis on religious practice. This is consistent with hierarchal cultures that place emphasis on obedience to elders and superiors.

By contrast, the Italian preschool teachers placed an emphasis on social integration, observance of social rules and autonomous identity. None of them mentioned religious practice, and little importance was ascribed to respect for adults, sense of family and original culture.

This and other studies provide strong empirical evidence that immigrant families have divergent development goals to their host nation educators. The different goals between the two groups reflect different beliefs about what is important in fostering a child's development and preparing them for their adult life.

The studies described in this chapter are part of a growing body of research confirming that children's early cognitive development reflects the environment in which they are raised. The activities that children are engaged in and the interactions with parents, siblings, peers and especially mothers, provide essential stimulation for cognitive development.

Notes

1 Sapolsky, R.M. (2017). *Behave: The Biology of Humans at our Best and Worst.* London: Penguin, p. 269.

2 Brain Architecture (n.d.). Harvard University Centre on the Developing Child. Downloaded from https://developingchild.harvard.edu/science/key-concepts/brain-architecture/ on 24 May 2019.
3 Gopnik, A., Meltzoff, A.N., & Kuhl, P.K. (1999). *The Scientist in the Crib: Minds, Brains, and How Children Learn*. New York: William Morrow & Co.
4 Ibid.
5 Kolb, B., & Gibb, R. (2011). Brain plasticity and behaviour in the developing brain. *Journal of the Canadian Academy of Child and Adolescent Psychiatry, 20*(4), 265. Downloaded from https://www.ncbi.nlm.nih.gov/pmc/articles/PMC3222570/ on 24 May 2019.
6 Ibid.
7 Ibid.
8 Brain architecture (n.d.).
9 Ibid.
10 Greenough, W.T., & Chang, F.F. (1989). Plasticity of synapse structure and pattern in the cerebral cortex. In A. Peters & E.G. Jones (Eds.), *Cerebral Cortex*, vol. 7. New York: Plenum Press, pp. 391–440; Sirevaag, A.M., & Greenough, W.T. (1987). A multivariate statistical summary of synaptic plasticity measures in rats exposed to complex, social and individual environments. *Brain Research, 441*, 386–392.
11 Kolb & Gibb (2011).
12 Kolb, B. (1990). *Brain Plasticity and Behavior*. Mahwah, NJ: Erlbaum.
13 Kolb & Gibb (2011).
14 Ibid.; and Myers, M.M., Brunelli, S.A., Squire, J.M., Shindledecker, R., & Hofer, M.A. (1989). Maternal behavior of SHR rats in its relationship to offspring blood pressure. *Developmental Psychobiology, 22*, 29–53.
15 Leyendecker, B., Jäkel, J., Kademoğlu, S.O., & Yagmurlu, B. (2011). Parenting practices and pre-schoolers' cognitive skills in Turkish immigrant and German families. *Early Child Development and Care, 181*(8), 1095–1110, p. 1095.
16 Arnold, D., & Doctoroff, G.L. (2003). The early education of socioeconomically disadvantaged children. *Annual Review of Psychology*, 54, 517–545. Krajewski, K., Schneider, W., & Nieding, G. (2008). Zur Bedeutung von Arbeitsgedächtnis, Intelligenz, phonologischer Bewusstheit und früher Mengen-Zahlen-Kompetenz beim Übergang vom Kindergarten in die Grundschule [The importance of working memory, cognitive performance, phonological awareness and early numeracy competence at the transition from Kindergarten to first grade]. *Psychologie in Erziehung und Unterricht, 55*, 100–113; NICHD Early Child Care Research Network. (2005). Predicting individual differences in attention, memory and planning in first graders from experiences at home, child care, and school. *Developmental Psychology, 41*, 99–114; Rimm-Kaufman, S. E., & Pianta, R.C. (2000). An ecological perspective on the transition to Kindergarten: A theoretical framework to guide empirical research. *Journal of Applied Developmental Psychology, 21*, 491–511; Schneider, W., Knopf, M., & Sodian, B. (2008). Verbal memory development from early childhood to early adulthood. In W. Schneider & M. Bullock (Eds.), *Human Development from Early Childhood to Early Adulthood: Evidence from the Munich Longitudinal Study on the Genesis of Individual Competencies (LOGIC)*. Abingdon: Routledge, pp. 113–129.
17 Lavelli, M., Döge, P., & Bighin, M. (2016). Socialization goals of immigrant mothers from diverse cultures and of their children's preschool teachers in Italy. *Journal of Cross-Cultural Psychology, 47*(2), 197–214.
18 Bradley, R.H. (2002). Environment and parenting. *Handbook of Parenting, 2*, 281–314; Arnold & Doctoroff (2003).
19 Bourdieu, P. (1977). Cultural reproduction and social reproduction. In J. Karabel & A. H. Halsey (Eds.), *Power and Ideology in Education*. New York: Oxford University Press, pp. 487–511.

20 Tamis-LeMonda, C.S., Shannon, J.D., Cabrera, N.J., & Lamb, M.E. (2004). Fathers and mothers at play with their 2- and 3-year-olds: Contributions to language and cognitive development. *Child Development, 75*, 1806–1820; Williams, W.M., & Sternberg, R.J. (2002). How parents can maximize children's cognitive abilities. In M.H. Bornstein (Ed.), *Handbook of Parenting*, vol. 5. Mahwah, NJ: Erlbaum, 169–194.

21 Carra, C., Lavelli, M., & Keller, H. (2014). Differences in practices of body stimulation during the first 3 months: Ethnotheories and behaviors of Italian mothers and West African immigrant mothers. *Infant Behavior and Development, 37*(1), 5–15.

22 Bornstein, M.H. (1989). Between caretakers and their young: Two modes of interaction and their consequences for cognitive growth. In M.H. Bornstein & J.S. Bruner (Eds.), *Interaction in Human Development: Behavioural and Biological Perspectives.* Hillsdale, NJ: Erlbaum, pp. 147–170; Pomerleau, A., Malcuit, G., & Sabatier, C. (1991). Childrearing practices and parental beliefs in three cultural groups of Montréal: Québécois, Vietnamese, Haitian. In M.H. Bornstein (Ed.), *Cultural Approaches to Parenting.* Hillsdale, NJ: Erlbaum, pp. 45–68; Shweder, R.A., Goodnow, J., Hatano, G., LeVine, R.A., Markus, H., & Miller, P. (1998). The cultural psychology of development: One mind, many mentalities. In R.M. Lerner (Ed.), *Handbook of Child Psychology, Vol. 1: Theoretical Models of Human Development*, 5th edition. New York: Wiley, pp. 865–937.

23 Harkness, S., Super, C.M., & van Tijen, N. (2000). Individualism and the 'Western mind' reconsidered: American and Dutch parents' ethnotheories of the child. In R. Harkness, C. Raeff, & C.M. Super (Eds.), Variability in the social construction of the child. *New Directions for Child and Adolescent Development, 87*, 23–39; Stewart, S.M., Bond, M.H., Deeds, O., & Chung, S.F. (1999). Intergenerational patterns of values and autonomy expectations in cultures of relatedness and separateness. *Journal of Cross-cultural Psychology, 30*, 575–593.

24 LeVine, R.A., Dixon, S., LeVine, S., Richman, A., Leiderman, P.H., Keefer, C.H., & Brazelton, T.B. (1994). *Child Care and Culture: Lessons from Africa.* New York: Cambridge University Press.

25 Ibid.

26 Greenfield, P.M., & Suzuki, L. (1998). Culture and human development: Implications for parenting, education, pediatrics, and mental health. In I.E. Sigel & K.A. Renninger (Eds.), *Handbook of Child Psychology: Vol. 4: Child Psychology in Practice*, 5th edition. New York: Wiley, pp. 1059–1109; Shweder et al. (1998).

27 Falladé, S. (1960). Le développement psycho-moteur de l'enfant Africain du Sénégal. *Concours Médical, 82*, 1005–1013.

28 LeVine, R.A., & LeVine, S.E. (1963). *Nyansongo: A Gusii community in Kenya.* New York: Wiley.

29 Bril, B., & Sabatier, C. (1986). The cultural context of motor development: Postural manipulations in the daily life of Bambora babies (Mali). *International Journal of Behavioural Development, 9*, 439–453.

30 Harkness, S., & Super, C.M. (2001) Culture and parenting. In M.H. Bornstein (Ed.), *Handbook of Parenting.* Hillsdale, NJ: Erlbaum, pp. 253–280.

31 Keller, H., Yovsi, R.D., &, Völker, S. (2002). The role of motor stimulation in parental ethnotheories: The case of Cameroonian Nso and German women. *Journal of Cross-Cultural Psychology, 33*, 398–414; Keller, H., Abels, M., Lamm, B., Yovsi, R.D., Völker, S., & Lakhani, A. (2005). Ecocultural effects on early infant care: A study in Cameroon, India, and Germany. *Ethos, 33*, 512–541.

32 Carra et al. (2014).

33 Ibid., p. 5.

34 Lamm, B., Keller, H., Yovsi, R.D., & Chaudary, N. (2008). Grandmaternal and maternal ethnotheories about early child care. *Journal of Family Psychology, 22*, 80–88.

35 Keller, H., Miranda, D., & Gauda, G. (1984). The naive theory of the infant and some maternal attitudes. A two-country study. *Journal of Cross-Cultural Psychology*, 15, 165–179.

36 Keller, H., & Zach, U. (1993). Developmental consequences of early eye contact behaviour. *Acta Paedopsychiatrica*, 56, 31–36. Keller, H., Loewer, M., & Runde, B. (1990). Analyse spontaner Sprache von Eltern in Interaktionssituationen mit ihren Säuglingen und Kleinkindern: Entwicklungsveränderungen und kulturspezifische Aspekte [Analysis of spontaneous child directed speech in interactional situations between mothers and their small children: development and cultural aspects]. *Zeitschrift für Entwicklungspsychologie und Pädagogische Psychologie, 22*, 341–353.
37 Grossmann, K., Fremmer-Bombik, E., Rudolph, J., & Grossmann, K.E. (1988). Maternal attachment representations as related to patterns of infant–mother attachment and maternal care during the first year. In R.A. Hinde & J. Stevenson-Hinde (Eds.), *Relationships within Families.* Oxford: Oxford University Press, pp. 241–260.
38 Nsamenang, A.B. (1992). *Human Development in Cultural Context: A Third World Perspective.* Newbury Park, CA: Sage; Nsamenang, A.B., & Lamb, M.E. (1994). Socialization of Nso children in the Bamenda grassfields of Northwest Cameroon. In P. M. Greenfield & R.R. Cocking (Eds.), *Cross-cultural Roots of Minority Child Development.* Hillsdale, NJ: Erlbaum, pp. 133–146.
39 Ogunnaike, A. (1997). Yoruba toddlers: Relating cognitive performance to family sociodemographics and mediating factors in the child's environment. Unpublished doctoral dissertation. Medford, MA: Tufts University.
40 Keller, H., Völker, S., & Yovsi, R.D. (2005). Conceptions of parenting in different cultural communities: The case of West African Nso and Northern German women. *Social Development, 14*(1), 158–180.
41 Carra et al. (2014).
42 Ibid., p. 11.
43 Ibid.
44 Leyendecker et al. (2011).
45 Biedinger, N. (2010). Early ethnic inequality: The influence of social background and parental involvement on preschool children's cognitive ability in Germany. *Child Indicators Research, 3*(1), 11–28.
46 Becker, R., & Lauterbach, W. (2004). Vom Nutzen vorschulischer Kinderbetreuung für Bildungschancen. In R. Becker & W. Lauterbach (Eds.), *Bildung als Privileg? Erklärungen und Befunde zu den Ursachen der Bildungsungleichheit.* Wiesbaden: VS Verlag für Sozialwissenschaften, pp. 127–159. Ditton, H., Krüsken, J., & Schauenberg, M. (2005). Bildungsungleichheit—Der Beitrag von Familie und Schule. *Zeitschrift für Erziehungswissenschaft, 8*(2), 285–30. Driessen, G.W.J.M. (2001). Ethnicity, forms of capital, and educational achievement. *International Review of Education, 47*(6), 513–538.
47 Beidinger (2010).
48 Göncü, A. (1993). Guided participation in Keciören. In B. Rogoff, J. Mistry, A. Göncü, & C. Mosier (Eds.), *Guided Participation in Cultural Activities by Toddlers and Caregivers.* Monographs of the Society for Research in Child Development; Serial No. 236, vol. 58. Chicago, IL: Chicago University Press, pp. 126–147. Göncü, A., Mistry, J., & Mosier, C. (2000). Cultural variations in the play of toddlers. *International Journal of Behavioral Development, 24*, 321–329.
49 Citlak, B., Leyendecker, B., Schräpler, K., & Schölmerich, A. (2010). "Bildungserwartungen beim Übergang in die Grundschule – Ein Vergleich von deutschen und zugewanderten Eltern [Educational aspirations of immigrant parents at the start of school – A comparison of German and immigrant parents]".
50 Beidinger (2010), p. 25.
51 Leyendecker et al. (2011).
52 Nauck, B., & Özel, S. (1986). Erziehungsvorstellungen und Sozialisationspraktiken in türkischen Migrantenfamilien. *Zeitschrift für Sozialisationsforschung und Erziehungssoziologie, 6*(2), 285–312; Wittmann, G. (1990). *Soziale Kompetenz im Kindergarten: Eine Explorationsstudie mit türkischen und Deutschen Kindern.* München: Profil-Verlag.

53 Espy, K.A., Molfese, V.J., & DiLalla, L.F. (2001). Effects of environmental measures on intelligence in young children: Growth curve modelling of longitudinal data. *Merrill-Palmer Quarterly, 47*(1), 42–73.
54 Moscardino, U., Bertelli, C., & Altoè, G. (2011). Culture, migration, and parenting: A comparative study of mother-infant interaction and childrearing patterns in Romanian, Romanian immigrant and Italian families. *International Journal of Developmental Science, 5*(1–2), 11–25.
55 Moscardino, U., Nwobu, O., & Axia, G. (2006). Cultural beliefs and practices related to infant health and development among Nigerian immigrant mothers in Italy. *Journal of Reproductive and Infant Psychology, 24*, 241–255, p. 251.
56 Lavelli, Döge, & Bighin (2016).
57 Ministero dell'Istruzione, dell'Università e della Ricerca. (2012). Indicazioni nazionali per il curricolo della scuola dell'infanzia e del primo ciclo d'istruzione [National curriculum for preschool and primary school]. Retrieved from http://www.indicazioninazionali.it/documenti_Indicazioni_nazionali/indicazioni_nazionali_infanzia_primo_ciclo.pdf.
58 Rosenthal, M.K. (1999). Out-of-home child care research: A cultural perspective. *International Journal of Behavioral Development*, 23, 477–451.
59 Tobin, J., Arzubiaga, A.E., & Adair, J.K. (2013). Children crossing borders: Immigrant parent and teacher perspectives on preschool. New York: Russell Sage; Gaitanides, S. (2007). 'Man müsste mehr voneinander wissen!' Umgang mit kultureller Vielfalt im Kindergarten ['We should know more about each other!' *Coping with cultural diversity in kindergarten*]. Frankfurt, Germany: Fachhochschulverlag.
60 Lavelli, Döge, & Bighin (2016).
61 Ibid.

7 Human capital, cognitive skills and cultural change

> My desire for them is to have a high level of education but I don't know what sort of support I should give my children
>
> Samoan Mother living in New Zealand[1]

Economics is the science of resource use, and the previous chapters revealed that the resource base has a huge influence on people's values, motivations and beliefs. It also determines the capabilities needed to prosper with those resources. Since the 1960s, economists have shown great interest in the skills and knowledge that people possess. They discovered that this 'human capital' is a very important influence on the level of prosperity (or poverty) that a society experiences.

The concept of human capital became popular among economists with the publication of influential papers by Schultz (1961), Becker (1964), and Mincer (1970, 1974).[2] This spawned growing research in the area, with an emerging focus on how achievement is related to school inputs, families, and other factors such as neighbourhoods, peers or general institutional structure.[3] Neilsen (2017) notes that human capital theory is

> the dominant paradigm economists use to understand labour income and inequality at the individual level …[4]

This theory states that the skills and attributes possessed by a worker is a form of capital that determines their income. Economists see it as an enormously useful framework for understanding phenomena including labour earnings and inequality.[5] Under this approach, a person with low skills is likely to earn less than someone with more skills.

Sadly, some social scientists have ignored the work of economists seeing it as a deficit-oriented discourse. Economists acknowledge that human capital theory does not explain all income variance but it is a very important influence. Hence, Human Capital theory and the contents of this book are not a challenge to structural explanations but are a complement.

The connection between cognitive skills and income has been well documented by economists, and has been researched using a number of different methods. As far back as 1976, Wachtel studied the incomes of World War Two veterans and their scores on military tests.[6] He found a positive correlation. In a longitudinal study of baby boomers in the United States, Zagorsky (2007) found that 'each point increase in IQ test scores raises income by between $234 and $616 per year'.[7] He also discovered that financial distress is also linked to IQ scores.

Lynn, Vanhanen and Stuart (2002) studied the link at a national level.[8] In their book *IQ and the Wealth of Nations*, the authors noted that the intelligence of populations is a major factor in the difference in economic growth and per capita income gaps between rich and poor people.

Ethnic comparisons within the United States have also been conducted. For example, Nyborg and Jenson (2011) studied military veterans and found that black veterans had similar incomes and job status to whites when IQ test scores were held constant.[9] The research also provides us with some level of optimism. For example, Johnson and Neal (1998) found that black women earned 5% more per hour than similarly aged white women with the same IQ scores.[10] This raises the hope that improving cognitive ability could have a positive impact on the earnings of ethnic minorities.

To augment our optimism, James Flynn (2009) has found that cognitive levels, as measured by IQ tests are improving.[11] Most encouraging, a study by Dickens and Flynn (2006) found that the scores of black people are improving very fast.[12] In fact, the difference between black people and white people closed by about five or six IQ points between 1972 and 2002.

Studies by labour economists have confirmed the importance of cognitive skills. Following an analysis of jobs by Acemoglu and Autor (2011), labour economists began to classify jobs along two dimensions.[13] The first dimension is the extent to which a job is based on manual or cognitive skills. The second dimension is the extent to which a job is routine or non-routine. By routine, they mean the extent to which a task can be codified by a set of instructions and undertaken by a machine. Routine manual jobs tend to be blue-collar jobs while routine-cognitive are white-collar jobs. A non-routine task would be too complex to write a simple set of instructions for as there may be many variables and they may also change. They involve abstract tasks that require problem-solving skills, adaptability and creativity.

Non-routine-cognitive jobs normally require the highest skills while routine manual jobs tend to be low-skilled. The problem is, in recent decades many skills have been replaced by machine and computers or transferred to low-wage nations. This trend is unlikely to diminish yet it has a significant impact on earnings.

A large body of literature now confirms that human capital is one of the most important factors contributing to economic growth and wealth creation.[14] It does this through improvements in labour productivity and by increasing the rate of innovation and diffusion of technology.[15] Similarly, as a sector grows in technological complexity, it places greater demands on the education level of its workforce.[16]

The importance of schooling has been emphasised and became a central element of development strategies both by international organisations and national governments. However, growth in school attainment is not always matched with improved economic conditions.[17] Measures of the quality of schooling have revealed little relationship with growth. Measures such as that used by UNESCO include pupil/teacher ratio, percentage of female teachers, percentage of trained teachers, public expenditure on primary education as a percentage of GDP, and public expenditure per pupil on primary education.[18] However, these measures do not correlate well with economic growth. Despite the strong focus on human capital, gaps between developed and developing countries remain. Some countries, for example Latvia, Chile and Brazil, have made significant gains but overall, developing countries have made little gain on developed countries.[19]

Part of the problem appears to be the relevance of what is taught in schools. Not all schooling contributes to economic growth and some content has little if any impact on growth. Hence, Eric Hanushek argues that the emphasis should be less on school attainment per se, and more on cognitive skills. He notes 'Cognitive skills of the population – rather than mere school attainment – are powerfully related to individual earnings, to the distribution of income, and most importantly to economic growth.'[20]

Drawing on internationally administered tests, Hanushek and Woessmann (2012) found a stronger correlation between economic growth and cognitive skills. In fact, their findings suggest that 'conditional on initial income levels, regional growth over the last four decades is completely described by differences in cognitive skills'.[21] The authors do not rule out the possibility of reverse causation, that is, economic growth facilitates better schooling, but even this does not negate their findings as we could expect a more reflexive relationship between cognitive skills and earnings. Wealthier nations with more advanced technologies would need workers with greater cognitive ability and this would impact on educational demands. The process may well be one of both push and pull.

The relationship between cognitive skills and earnings was also found in migrants. Despite whatever disadvantages they may have on arrival, when people from developing nations migrate to developed nations, they become more productive (and earn more) as their labour is combined with more capital than in their home nation. They are also working in a more efficient institutional set-up. Hence the marginal product of their labour increases.[22] Where jobs exist, migrants can earn more in their new country than they did at home, even though they possess the same human capital. However, if the skills and knowledge that they possess are not matched with the new economy, migrants are likely to be employed at lower income levels which contributes to their poverty.

A body of evidence reveals that the human capital developed in one country cannot always be readily translated to a new country.[23] In such cases, the immigrant suffers human capital devaluation with many skills and much knowledge being of no use in the receiving society.[24] The most important of these skills is language.[25]

If over successive generations, the immigrating ethnic group modifies its capabilities, this can enable them to earn higher wages. However, if it doesn't, we may see inter-generational poverty. This raises questions about the pace of cultural change. Roland (2005) states that cultures can be very slow to change.[26]

There are several reasons for this. First is the natural tendency of parents to teach their children what they have learned from their own parents. A second form of inertia comes from organisations that reinforce the existing culture, such as churches or tribal structures. Finally, if an ethnic group has high fertility, their cultural behaviours can spread rapidly despite being economically inefficient.[27]

Lamont and Small (2010) do not accept that cultures are static to the point that they cause poverty.[28] For example, Jiménez and Fitzgerald (2007) noted that Mexican immigrants and their descendants living in the United States, are on many measures more similar to other Americans than they are to Mexicans living in Mexico.[29] This includes educational achievement. However, there is still an educational lag with performance behind other ethnic groups. This study shows that cultures are capable of change, but raises questions over the rate of change.

Most scholars accept that a group's culture is affected by outside forces, but there are genuine disagreements about the durability of cultural content.[30] This book suggests that academics and policy-makers need to go beyond discussions over whether cultures are capable of change. Studies are needed on what aspects of culture are necessary to eliminate poverty; that is, which behaviours generate wealth and what are the barriers to acquiring those behaviours?

This discussion lends itself to scholarship from evolutionary economics which examines how economies evolve over time. Evolutionary economics views economic behaviour differently to mainstream economics. Mainstream economics has traditionally seen people as rational agents, from which we would expect them to acquire behaviours that maximised resource use. In contrast, evolutionary economics presented an alternative view and more closely considered how best practice techniques and behaviours are acquired by a population. It recognises that what is considered best practice depends on the environment the person is in.

The seminal work in evolutionary economics is Nelson and Winter's (1982) *An Evolutionary Theory of Economic Change* [31] which studied companies and argued that the business with the most effective behaviours will become profitable and this will signal to other companies that they too should acquire those behaviours. They called these behaviours 'routines'. However, they also noted that behavioural patterns or routines do not flexibly respond to changes in the environment. The daily routines that people perform are like genes and restrict flexibility. If a firm persists with the old routines, it is likely to go out of business.

A focus of evolutionary economics is the acquisition of best practice behaviours. If a business succeeds with a new behaviour, other companies can hear of their new practices through a number of means, including suppliers or by headhunting workers who can introduce those practices. However, evolutionary economics recognises that people do not always behave rationally and a number of barriers to change exist.

This form of analysis can be applied to culture and families. If people want higher incomes, we would expect them to adopt the best behaviours, including parental behaviour. Charles Super (1976) study of parental practices among the Kipsigis provided a brief introduction to the importance of economies in the process of cultural transition.[32] In their traditional homelands, parental training had a strong focus on motor skills, but Super also studied 18 children whose families lived in European houses in the city of Nairobi, Kenya. Their fathers all had modern economy jobs, that is accountants, military officers, government and commercial administrators. Super found that their parental practices had become more American. Nevertheless, half the mothers continued their traditional parental practices of teaching their babies to sit and walk. Parental practices do not change overnight as the economic and cultural base changes.

Another example of parenting practices in new economic systems occurs when families migrate. Moscardino, Nwobu and Axia (2006) studied the practices of Nigerian mothers who had immigrated to Italy.[33] As in other parts of Africa, the importance of motor development is stressed in Nigeria.[34] Nigerian mothers use different exercises to stimulate their children's motor development. From the age of 2, this may include fetching objects or doing chores.[35] At an earlier age, it will include exercises, massages and motor games.[36]

Moscardino, Nwobu and Axia (2006) found that the same parental practices were used when the families immigrated to Italy.[37] Like mothers everywhere, the Nigerian mothers showed concern for their children's development, but the emphasis was solidly on motor skills with milestones of development noted. Mothers had precise ideas of the ages at which a baby would learn to sit (4–5 months), to crawl (6–7 months) and walk (9–10 months). By their first birthday, they would be expected to walk without any assistance from an adult. As one mother said:

> It's our own culture that by this stage the child should learn to crawl, 'cause before 1 year you have to be fit ... by the time he's completing his 1 year, he should be able to stand, move around by himself without anybody holding him. So by then I'll be training him to learn to crawl, move his body.[38]

Reasons for differences in development were noted. Mothers expressed concern that the smaller environment and colder climate did not allow their children to practise their motor skills as they could in Nigeria. Different development goals reflected the different environments. Nigerians were guided by the need to promote the physical health of their children, but also infant autonomy. The emphasis was 'survival, health and physical growth' to protect the baby from disease and other environmental risks found in Africa. Children were also taught socially accepted modes of interacting in Nigerian communities.

The Nigerians did adopt some practices of Italian parenting, under advice from Italian doctors or paediatricians, or perhaps because African baby products were not available in Africa. This illustrates that cultural change did occur, but overall, there was a persistence of cultural parental practices.

The fact that Nigerian mothers generally retained their traditional practices is consistent with other studies. As Le Vine (1988) noted, belief systems regarding child-rearing and socialisation are among the cultural beliefs that are most resistant to change.[39] That is not to say that change does not occur as contact with the new culture proceeds, and different aspects of parenting may change at different rates.[40] Nevertheless, there is a strong persistence of parental beliefs acquired from their parents in their country of origin.

Children are a family's biggest investment so it is no surprise that there may be resistance to change from established patterns. However, it is not the only barrier to change. For example, parental behaviours occur within families, so can be harder to observe. One wonders how the Nigerian migrants could have gained knowledge of the new behaviours of doctors and paediatricians had not advised them.

This raises the possibility of another barrier to success; that is, you cannot adopt a behaviour if you don't know it exists. In order to acquire a behaviour, you must have exposure and understanding of that behaviour. To put it another way, success is limited if 'you don't know what you don't know'.

If parents cannot learn new behaviours, they will continue with the socialisation practices they know best. The old behaviours are passed on to the next generation in a manner consistent with Nelson and Winter's view of routines as genes. The consequence is the ethnic group is left without the behaviours necessary to deliver socio-economic success in a modern knowledge economy.

There are other reasons why successful behaviours might not be adopted. It is possible that an ethnic group may not be aware of the importance of wealth generating behaviours, or alternatively do not know how to engage in those behaviours. Finally, there is the issue raised in our discussion on assimilation. The ethnic group may not want greater material wealth. In which case, the elimination of poverty can, in itself, be criticised for promoting Western values.

Notes

1 Amituanai-Toloa, M., McNaughton, S., Lai, M.K., & Airini. (2009). Milestone 4, Pasifika Schooling Improvement Project. Unpublished draft report to the Ministry of Education, Wellington, p. 17.
2 Schultz, T.W. (1961). Investment in human capital. *American Economic Review, 51* (March (1)), 1–17; Becker, G.S. (1964). *Human Capital: A Theoretical and Empirical Analysis, with Special Reference to Education.* New York: National Bureau of Economic Research; Mincer, J. (1970). The distribution of labor incomes: A survey with special reference to the human capital approach. *Journal of Economic Literature, 8* (March (1)), 1–26; Mincer, J. (1974). *Schooling, Experience, and Earnings.* New York: NBER.
3 Hanushek, E.A. (2013). Economic growth in developing countries: The role of human capital. *Economics of Education Review, 37*, 204–212.
4 Nielsen, E.R. (2017). Human capital and wealth before and after capital in the 21st century. In H. Boushey J.B. Delong, & M. Steinbaum (Eds.). *After Piketty: The Agenda for Economics and Inequality.* Cambridge, MA: Harvard University Press, pp. 150–169, p.151.
5 Ibid.
6 Wachtel, P. (1976). The effect on earnings of school and college investment expenditures. *The Review of Economics and Statistics*, 326–331.
7 Zagorsky, J.L. (2007). Do you have to be smart to be rich? The impact of IQ on wealth, income and financial distress. *Intelligence, 35*(5), 489–501.
8 Lynn, R., Vanhanen, T., & Stuart, M. (2002). *IQ and the Wealth of Nations.* Westport, CT: Greenwood Publishing Group.

9 Nyborg, H., & Jensen, A.R. (2001). Occupation and income related to psychometric g. *Intelligence, 29*(1), 45–55.
10 Johnson, W.R., & Neal, D.A. (1997). *Basic Skills and the Black–White Earnings Gap.* University of Virginia, Thomas Jefferson Center for Political Economy.
11 Flynn, J.R. (2009). *What is Intelligence: Beyond the Flynn Effect.* Cambridge.
12 Dickens, W.T., & Flynn, J.R. (2006). Black Americans reduce the racial IQ gap: Evidence from standardization samples. *Psychological Science, 17*(10), 913–920.
13 Acemoglu, D., & Autor, D. (2011). Skills, tasks and technologies: Implications for employment and earnings. In O. Ashenfelter & D. Card (Eds.), *Handbook of Labor Economics*, vol. 4. Amsterdam: Elsevier, pp. 1043–1171.
14 Lucas, R. (1988). On the mechanics of economic development, *Journal of Monetary Economics, 22*, 3–42; Mankiw, N.G., Romer, D., & Weil, D.N. (1992). Contribution to the empirics of economic growth. *The Quarterly Journal of Economics, 107*(2), 407–437.
15 Pistorius, C. (2004). The Competitiveness and innovation. *Elektron, 21*(3); Siggel, E. (2001). India's trade policy reforms and competitiveness industry in the 1980s. *World Economy, 24*(2), 159–183; Siggel, E. (2000). *Uganda's policy Reforms, Competitiveness and Regional Integration Industry: A Comparison with Kenya. African Economic Policy.* Discussion paper 24; Washington: United States Agency for International Development: Bureau for Africa; Horwitz, F. (2005). HR can competitiveness advance. *Executive Business Brief, 10*, 50–52.
16 Mincer, J. (1995). *Economic Development, Growth of Human Capital, and the Dynamics of the Wage Structure, 1994–95.* Discussion Paper Series No. 744 (September), Columbia University, p. 38.
17 Easterly, W. (2001). *The Elusive Quest for Growth: An Economist's Adventures and Misadventures in the Tropics.* Cambridge, MA: The MIT Press; Pritchett, L. (2006). Does learning to add up add up? The returns to schooling in aggregate data. In E.A. Hanushek & F. Welch (Eds.), *Handbook of the Economics of Education.* Amsterdam: North Holland, pp. 635–695.
18 Hanushek, E.A. (2003). The failure of input-based schooling policies. *Economic Journal, 113*(485), F64–F98; Hanushek (2013).
19 Hanushek, E.A., & Woessmann, L. (2012). Do better schools lead to more growth? Cognitive skills, economic outcomes, and causation. *Journal of Economic Growth, 17* (4), 267–321.
20 Hanushek (2013), p. 204.
21 Hanushek & Woessmann (2012), p. 268.
22 Olson, M. (1996). Distinguished lecture on economics in government: Big bills left on the sidewalk: Why some nations are rich, and others poor. *The Journal of Economic Perspectives, 10*(2), 3–24.
23 Chiswick (1978).
24 Friedberg, R.M. (2000). You can't take it with you? Immigrant assimilation and the portability of human capital. *Journal of Labor Economics, 18*, 221–251.
25 Kristen et al. (2011).
26 Roland, G. (2005). Understanding institutional change: Fast moving and slow moving institutions. Working paper. Downloaded from http://emlab.berkeley.edu/users/groland/pubs/gr3.pdf.
27 Giuso et al. (2006).
28 Lamont, M., & Small, M.L. (2010). Cultural diversity and anti-poverty policy. *International Social Science Journal, 61*, 169–180.
29 Jiménez, T.R., & Fitzgerald, D. (2007). Mexican Assimilation. *Du Bois Review: Social Science and Research on Race, 4*, 337–354.
30 Vaisey, S. (2010). What people want: Rethinking poverty, culture, and educational attainment. *The Annals of the American Academy of Political and Social Science, 629*, 75–101.

31 Nelson, R.R., & Winter, S.G. (1982). *An Evolutionary Theory of Economic Change.* Cambridge MA: Harvard University Press.
32 Super, C.M. (1976). Environmental effects on motor development: The case of 'African infant precocity'. *Developmental Medicine & Child Neurology, 18*(5), 561–567.
33 Moscardino, U., Nwobu, O., & Axia, G. (2006). Cultural beliefs and practices related to infant health and development among Nigerian immigrant mothers in Italy. *Journal of Reproductive and Infant Psychology, 24*(3), 241–255.
34 Zeitlin, M. (1996). 'My child is my crown': Yoruba parental theories and practices in early childhood. In S. Harkness & C.M. Super (Eds.), *Parents' Cultural Belief Systems: Their Origins, Expressions, and Consequences.* New York: Guilford Press, pp. 407–427.
35 Aina, T.A., Agiobu-Kemmer, I., Etta, E.F., Zeitlin, M.F., & Setiloane, K. (1993). *Early Childhood Care, Development and Nutrition in Lagos State, Nigeria.* New York: UNICEF. Phase 1 Survey Results from the Positive Deviance in Nutrition Research Project, Faculty of Social Sciences, University of Lagos, and Tufts University School of Nutrition.
36 Moscardino, Nwobu, & Axia (2006).
37 Ibid.
38 Ibid, p. 251.
39 LeVine, R.A. (1988). Human parental care: Universal goals, cultural strategies, and individual behavior. In R.A. LeVine, P.M. Miller, & M.M. West (Eds.), *Parental Behavior in Diverse Societies.* San Francisco: Jossey-Bass, pp. 5–12.
40 Ngo, P.Y.L., & Malz, T.A. (1998). Cross-cultural and cross-generational differences in Asian American's cultural and family systems and their impact on academic striving. In H.I. McCubbin & E.A. Thompson (Eds.), *Resiliency in Family Series. Vol. 2: Resiliency in Native American and Immigrant Families.* Thousand Oaks, CA: Sage, pp. 265–274.

8 Blurred lines

Socio-economic status and ethnicity

The modern knowledge economy requires very different capabilities to those needed in a traditional resource-based economy. In a knowledge economy, a very important aspect of parenting is academic socialisation. The high importance attached to academic socialisation is a reflection of the specialised nature of careers and the need for ongoing learning.

Developmental and educational psychologists have conducted extensive research on the academic development of children and their work has revealed important differences between ethnic groups. Some readers of this book may feel uncomfortable with the notion that ethnic groups are compared in this way; however, the research is thorough, extensive and based on solid methodology. Hence, this book argues that developmental and educational psychologists can make an important contribution to solving poverty.

This is a sensitive area and, in writing this book, much consideration was given to appropriate terminology. For example, African Americans are commonly referred to as 'black'. For those of us living outside the United States, this terminology might seem offensive as it refers to an ethnic group by their skin colour. However, it is the preferred terminology. The rule of thumb used in this book is to use the same terminology as the material that is cited.

Academic success is of vital importance for future income streams. However, significant differences in education outcomes exist between ethnic groups, and these differences appear at a very young age. A number of studies have found that white children started kindergarten with significantly higher maths and reading scores than black and Latino children. The scores of Asian children were significantly higher than all.[1] The differences are so reliable that it justifies an examination of factors within specific racial/ethnic groups which impact on the child's skills.

Parental behaviour and family context are increasingly recognised as important for the educational development of children.[2] This includes parents' beliefs and expectations about education, as well as parental behaviours which impact on their children's academic and school-related development. Parental involvement can take a number of forms. It may include reading to children, academic expectations, communication on schooling matters, help with homework and any number of forms of support.

Given the importance of parenting for childhood development and the differences in parental practice between cultures, it would seem logical that academics explore the link between parenting and development outcomes. Some early exploration in this area included that done by Clark (1984) who examined how differences in parental style and education expectations affected academic achievement among African Americans.[3] Others included Steinberg (1996) and Kohn (1977) and Dornbusch and colleagues (1987).[4] They all found that varying parental practices and family processes had an important impact on a child's academic development.

However, this line of work did not receive a lot of attention as academics preferred to focus on the link between socio-economic status and academic disparities.[5] Influential work in this area was conducted by Pierre Bourdieu (1986), Kohn (1977) and Lareau (2002) who did not necessarily deny a role for ethnic differences but, their principal concern was social class and cultural capital accumulation.[6] Their findings stressed that the biggest difference in educational outcomes was not parental practice but socio-economic status.

Ethnic groups that perform poorly on academic outcomes are commonly groups with low socio-economic status and limited resources. Consequently, when researchers examine poor educational outcomes of different ethnic groups, their focus has been on economic resources.[7] Ethnicity and culture received little consideration.

The commonly held view is that ethnic minority families struggle, because of their low SES, to provide effective support for their children's academic development.[8] A large body of evidence has been presented to back up this view. There is a clear link between SES and the extent a family supports and invests in their children's academic development.

This can be seen in Figure 8.1. Poorer families have less time and resources to devote to their children. They are also more likely to be stressed which also impacts on the quality of their parenting. This in turn affects the academic development of their children who end up in low-paying jobs. Their low incomes mean, when they become parents, they achieve similar results as their parents. The result is a self-perpetuating poverty cycle. Under this view, culture and ethnicity plays no role in academic outcomes or incomes.

In recent years, a number of studies have revealed differing patterns of academic socialisation depending on families' ethnicity and culture.[9] However, given that many ethnic groups are also experiencing poverty, it is hard to determine whether the main cause of poor academic outcomes is poverty or ethnicity. As Yamamoto and Sonnenschein (2016) note:

> to what extent culture/ethnicity or SES plays a role in families' academic socialization and their children's academic trajectories is not clear. Because ethnicity and SES tend to be intertwined in the United States, it is often difficult to disentangle the effects of each element in the examination of academic socialization ...[10]

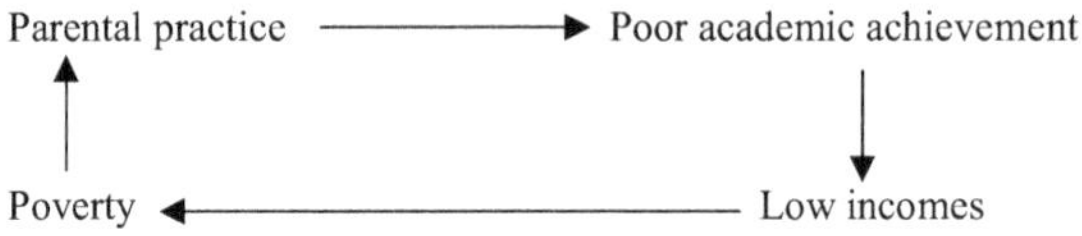

Figure 8.1 Poverty-based chain of causation.

The problem is that, in many instances, ethnicity and socio-economic status overlap. Research has 'not disentangled the influences of race, social class, and culture on family functioning and child development'.[11] There is limited information available on cultural characteristics and processes that underpin differences in parenting. The research suggests there are differences in parenting strategies between ethnic groups; however, it is less clear what those differences are.[12] Yet this information has strong implications in the choice of policy interventions and how they should be targeted.[13]

Nevertheless, a growing body of research is beginning to reveal important differences. All families from diverse ethnic and socio-economic backgrounds love and care for their children, but the ways in which they do so may differ.[14] This includes the practice and expression of parental warmth. Research has found that parents from lower socio-economic background and/or who are from ethnic minorities express less warmth towards their children.[15]

It may be that in some cases, culture is the main factor affecting parental practice and hence child outcomes. According to sociocultural theory, cultural beliefs, skills and values have a strong influence on family processes.[16] Learning is a socially determined process, and in the period before school, children rely on their parents to acquire their first cognitive skills.

Figure. 8.2 presents this alternative view in which inherited cultural practices may be the cause of poor academic achievement. In which case, it will also determine income levels when the child grows and the continued existence of intergenerational poverty.

A number of studies have already examined differences in parental practice between ethnic groups. For example, Sonnenschein, Metzger and Thompson (2016) noted the high prevalence of reading and maths difficulties among black and Latino children.[17] With this in mind, they studied parents' beliefs about reading and maths socialisation, frequency of children's engagement in reading and maths, and children's skills in those areas. They found significant differences, highlighting the importance of parental beliefs and practices for children's reading and maths outcomes.

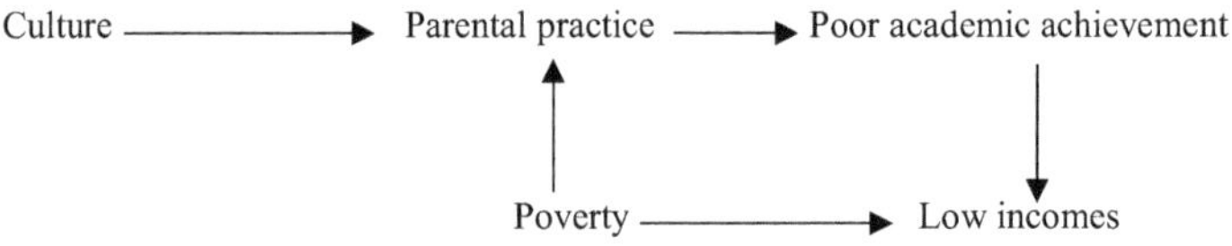

Figure 8.2 Chain of causation with culture as a determining factor.

Sonnenschein and Sun (2017) suggest that there are racial/ethnic differences in parents' academic socialisation.[18] They argued that race and ethnicity influences preschool enrichment activities, home literacy activities and parent's knowledge of children's development. This in turn influences their reading and maths skills by the time they get to kindergarten. Sonnenschein and Sun stress the need to consider 'the importance of heritage influences and the larger social structure when examining children's learning experiences and related family practices'.[19]

For example, Cheadle and Amato (2011) found that black families were less likely to engage in concerted cultivation of their children than white families.[20] Sonnenschein and Sun suggest that these differences 'may reflect differences in their views about how to interact with children and what activities to provide them (i.e. concerted cultivation) and/or may reflect differences in parents' knowledge about children's development ...'.[21] They found that whites and Asians engaged in home literacy activities significantly more frequently than blacks or Latinos. Whites also engaged in enrichment activities significantly more frequently than Asians, blacks or Latinos, however the effect of enrichment is more likely to impact on world knowledge and not impact on reading and maths scores.

Another important factor is the amount of time that parents spend with children. The widely held belief is that the more time that parents spend with their children, the better it is for their development. Studies have supported the notion that black and Hispanic parents spend less time in parenting activities than white parents.[22] However, less information is available on how that varies as the children age. With this in mind, Patterson (2017) examined the amount of time that black and white children spent with their mothers at each age between birth and age 14 years.[23] He found that, in the first years of their life, black children spend significantly less time with their mothers than their white counterparts. However, after the age of 14, difference between the races are reduced dramatically. From this he assumed that the black–white gap is unlikely to be driven by differences in parental time, once the child has entered school. However, the time spent in the preschool years is of importance.

To examine influences on child development, Todd and Wolpin (2007) constructed a composite measure of household involvement.[24] It included the number of books and musical instruments in the house, how often parents read to their children and the frequency with which the child reads for self-enjoyment. Other inclusions were whether the family receives a newspaper, visits museums or theatre, discusses television programmes, whether the child takes music lessons and how dangerous the interviewer perceived their home. Although this study could be criticised for having a bias towards performing arts, it nevertheless found that home inputs in early childhood accounted for 10–20% of the black–white test-score gap.

Brooks-Gunn and Markman (2005) examined seven different parental behaviours.[25] First was nurturance, which refers to the ways that love, affection and care are expressed. It reflects a level of warmth and sensitivity. Second was discipline which examines the parent's response when children engage in inappropriate behaviour. Third was teaching which refers to the conveying of information or skills to the child. Language was fourth, and refers to how extensively language is used between the parent and child. Materials refers to the cognitively and linguistically stimulating materials provided in the home. The sixth activity was monitoring and might otherwise be called 'keeping track' or watchfulness. Finally, management refers to the extent that events are scheduled in a structured household rhythm.

Their research found that there were several differences in parental behaviour and those differences are important for the child's school readiness. Notably, black and Hispanic mothers scored low on several behaviours. One of the most striking differences was language use with black and Hispanic mothers talking less to their young children than white mothers. This is of particular importance given that differences accumulate over time.

Another important difference was in nurturance. Blacks were more likely to be in the tough love group compared to whites. Black mothers were also rated as having lower levels of sensitivity. In terms of Baumrind's parenting styles, black mothers are more authoritarian and less authoritative than white mothers.

When they controlled for parenting differences, the racial and ethnic gaps for school readiness narrowed by 25–50%. This opens the possibility that changing parental behaviours could improve the school readiness of children from different ethnic groups. This is an exciting finding in that it implies the possibly that interventions could be introduced to change parental behaviour. The study's authors examined programmes that serve poor and minority families and found that programmes with a parenting component do improve parental skills in discipline, nurturance and talking to children.

It could be expected that more educated mothers might have better parenting skills, and research seems to draw this out. A large body of evidence has shown that parents with higher education and ability use better parental techniques. For example, the use of sophisticated problem resolution strategies has been linked to the level of ability of the mother.[26]

Kalil, Ryan and Corey (2012) found that college-educated mothers are more 'efficient' with their use of time and the way they tailored their activities depending on the stage of their child's development.[27] In particular, their time investments in care and play was greatest when their children were aged from birth to 2. Between the ages of 3 and 5, there was greater focus on teaching and learning activities including reading and problem-solving. From the age of 6 to 13, the focus was on parental management.

The differences between college-educated mothers and those that only had a high school education were greatest with the youngest children. This suggests that the more educated mothers may understand the greater importance of parental investments in early childhood for the child's development and success.

This emerging literature reveals that there are important differences in parenting that impact on a child's development. The problem is that our understanding of the ways in which ethnicity and socio-economic status impact on parenting is still very limited.[28] We cannot definitively pinpoint causation. There may even be variance between each ethnic group given their particular histories and cultures. It may be that a combination of historical factors is at play as shown in Figure 8.3. Until more evidence is available, we are left with an incomplete picture.

A body of research has emerged that is helping us see through these blurred lines. This research does not deny that poverty (nor ethnicity) is a factor, but seeks more knowledge on how it impacts on academic achievement. For example, Guo and Harris (2000) argue that it is not sufficient to say that incomes affect children's academic achievement.[29] This old explanation is too vague and does not reveal the causal pathways by which poverty works. Nielsen agrees:

> Researchers have not established a clear relationship between changes in parental resources and expenditures and changes in measure childhood academic achievement. The methodological obstacles that need to be overcome in this type of empirical work are simply very large.[30]

Guo and Harris considered the mediating factors through which poverty influences a child's intellectual development as shown in Figure.8.4. They found the influence of family poverty on children's intellectual development is mediated completely by the intervening mechanisms. Cognitive stimulation in the home was the most important mediating factor followed by parenting style, physical environment of the home, and child health at birth.

This has important implications for policy. Many existing interpretations assume that an increase an income will reduce poverty and hence lead to improvements in the child's cognitive development. However, research such as this reveals the relationship is more complicated. Guo and Harris argue that parenting style

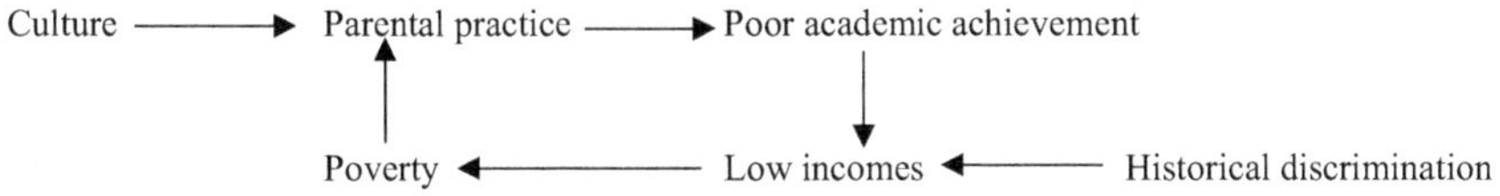

Figure 8.3 Chain of causation in which discrimination and culture both play a role.

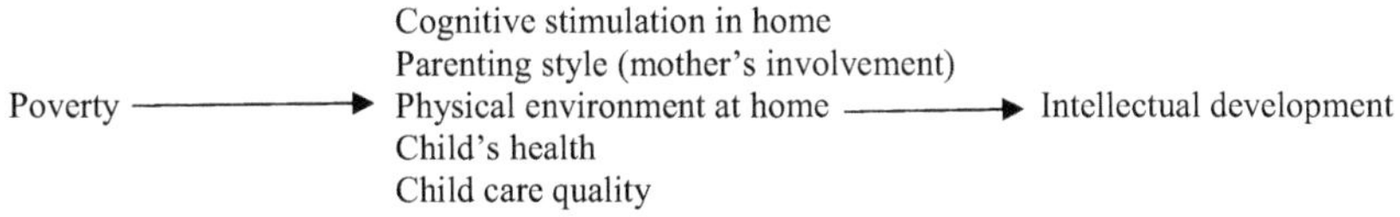

Figure 8.4 Mediating mechanisms of poverty on intellectual development.
Source: Adapted from Guo and Harris (2000)

cannot be shaped easily by material goods or services, and cannot be 'purchased' with additional income.

They conclude that 'Poverty has no direct effect on children's intellectual development' and that policy should focus on the intervening mechanisms that affect children's development. Such policies would be more effective than those based on income transfer. They do not deny, for example, that poverty affects cognitive stimulation and that cognitive stimulation effects intellectual development, but policies may be more effective targeting cognitive stimulation, not incomes. In other words, they advocate interventions that target the causal pathway through this process occurs. They suggest targeting children's cognitive environments and parenting behaviours is the most effective and less expensive intervention.

On a similar line, Ermisch (2008) sought to open the 'black box' to understand the mechanisms linking parents' socio-economic status and children's early cognitive and behavioural development.[31] In particular, he asked 'what do higher income parents do during the child's first three years that is conducive to better cognitive and behavioural outcomes?' This study examined parental activities such as reading at home, teaching the alphabet, painting and counting, teaching songs, poems and nursery rhymes. Consideration was also given to how often such activities were conducted. Parental style was also examined by questions, for example, that asked if there were a lot of rules, and are there regarding regular times for dinner, TV watching and bed, indicating a parental style with emphasis on structure.

The study found that an important part of the differences between parents with different income levels could be accounted for by 'what parents do'. The parents' educational activities and parenting style made an important contribution to the differences in cognitive and behavioural development. The study concludes:

> We might hesitate in concluding that 'what parents do with their children is more important than who they are' … but what parents do is important.[32]

Vonnie McLoyd (1998) did not deny the effect of poverty, but she too noted that the quality of parenting can overcome at least some of the effects of poverty. She notes that the 'link between socioeconomic disadvantage and children's socio-emotional functioning appears to be mediated partly by harsh, inconsistent parenting and elevated exposure to acute and chronic stressors'.[33]

Zimmermann and Vogler (2012) also found that good home environments appeared to overcome the barriers set by poor material circumstances.[34] In particular, they stressed the importance of providing stimulating and learning oriented experiences, and lesser so, parental encouragement. Notably they found a link between effective parenting and the mother's education. They suggest that education may provide mothers with knowledge, skills and self-confidence necessary for a happy marital relationship and successful child-rearing. They also acknowledge that coming from a poor background can make it harder for a parent to obtain a higher education. Nevertheless, the authors conclude with optimism:

The implications that material disadvantage can, at least partly be off-set by positive parental behaviors offers one ray of hope … parental warmth, involvement and moderate control.[35]

Notes

1 Lee, J.-S., & Bowen, N.K. (2006). Parent involvement, cultural capital, and the achievement gap among elementary school children. *American Educational Research Journal, 43*, 193–218. National Research Council (2009). In C.T. Cross, T.A. Woods, & H. Schweingruber (Eds.), *Mathematics Learning in Early Childhood: Paths Towards Excellence and Equity*. Washington, DC: The National Academies Press; Reardon, S.F., & Galindo, C. (2009). The Latino–White achievement gap in math and reading in the elementary grades. *American Educational Research Journal, 46*, 853–891.

2 Yamamoto, Y., & Sonnenschein, S. (2016). Family contexts of academic socialization: The role of culture, ethnicity, and socioeconomic status. *Research in Human Development, 13*(3), 183–190.

3 Clark, R.M. (1984). *Family Life and School Achievement: Why Poor Black Children Succeed or Fail*. Chicago, IL: University of Chicago Press.

4 Steinberg (1996); Kohn, M.L. (1977). *Class and Conformity: A Study in Values*. Chicago, IL: University of Chicago Press; Dornbusch, S.M., Ritter, P.L., Leiderman, H., Roberts, D.F., & Fraleigh, M.J. (1987). The relation of parenting style of adolescent school performance. *Child Development, 58*, 1244–1257.

5 Potter & Morris (2017).

6 Bourdieu, P. (1986). The forms of capital. In J.G. Richardson (Ed.), *Handbook of Theory and Research for the Sociology of Education*. New York: Greenwood, pp. 241–258; Kohn (1977); Lareau, A. (2002). Invisible inequality: Social class and childrearing in black families and white families. *American Sociological Review, 67*, 747–776.

7 Fryer & Levitt (2004). Duncan, G.J., & Murnane, R.J. (2011). *Whither Opportunity? Rising Inequality, Schools, and Children's Life Chances*. New York: Russell Sage.

8 Brooks-Gunn & Markman (2005); Lazar, A., & Slostad, F. (1999). How to overcome obstacles to parent–teacher partnerships. *The Clearing House: A Journal of Educational Strategies, Issues and Ideas, 72*(4), 206–210.

9 García Coll, C., & Marks, A.K. (2009). *Immigrant Stories: Ethnicity and Academics in Middle Childhood*. New York: Oxford University Press; Hill, N.E., Castellino, D.R., Lansford, J.E., Nowlin, P., Dodge, K.A., Bates, J.E., & Pettit, G.S. (2004). Parent academic involvement as related to school behavior, achievement, and aspirations: Demographic variations across adolescence. *Child Development, 75*, 1491–1509; Pomerantz, E., Ng, F.F.-Y., Cheung, C.S.-S., & Qu, Y. (2014). Raising happy children who succeed in school: Lessons from China and the United States. *Child Development Perspectives, 8*(2), 71–76; Yamamoto, Y., & Holloway, S.D. (2010). Parental expectations and children's academic performance in sociocultural context. *Educational Psychology Review, 22*, 189–214.

10 Yamamoto & Sonnenschein (2016).

11 Le et al. (2008).

12 McLoyd, V.C., Cauce, A.M., Takeuchi, D., & Wilson, L. (2000). Marital processes and parental socialization in families of color: A decade review of research. *Journal of Marriage and the Family, 62*(4), 1070–1093.

13 Le at al. (2008).

14 Hill, N.E., Bush, K.R., & Roosa, M.W. (2003). Relations between parenting and family socialization strategies and children's mental health: Low income, Mexican American and Euro-American mothers' and children's perspectives. *Child Development, 74*, 189–204; Mason, C.A., Walker-Barnes, C.J., Tu, S., Simons, J., & Martinez-Arrue,

R. (2004). Ethnic differences in the affective meaning of parental control behaviors. *Journal of Primary Prevention, 25*, 59–79.

15 Hoff-Ginsberg, Laursen, & Tardiff (2005); McLoyd, V.C. (1990). The impact of economic hardship on Black families and children: Psychological distress, parenting, and socioemotional development. *Child Development, 61*, 311–346; Pinderhughes E.E., Dodge, K.A., Bates, J.E., Petitt, G.S., & Zelli, A. (2000). Discipline responses: Influences of parents' socioeconomic status, ethnicity, beliefs about parenting, stress, and cognitive-emotional processes. *Journal of Family Psychology, 14*, 380–400.

16 Vygotsky, L.S. (1987). *The Collected Works of LS Vygotsky, Vol. 1: Problems of General Psychology, Including the Volume Thinking and Speech.* New York: Springer.

17 Sonnenschein, S., Metzger, S.R., & Thompson, J.A. (2016). Low-income parents' socialization of their preschoolers' early reading and math skills. *Research in Human Development, 13*(3), 207–224.

18 Sonnenschein, S., & Sun, S. (2017). Racial/ethnic differences in kindergartners' reading and math skills: Parents' knowledge of children's development and home-based activities as mediators. *Infant and Child Development, 26*(5), 1–21.

19 Ibid., p. 3.

20 Cheadle, J. E., & Amato, P. R. (2011). A quantitative assessment of Lareau's qualitative conclusions about class, race, and parenting. *Journal of Family Issues, 32*(5), 679–706.

21 Sonnenschein & Sun (2017), p. 3.

22 Kalil, A., Ryan, R., & Corey, M. (2012). Diverging destinies: Maternal education and the developmental gradient in time with children. *Demography, 49*(4), 1361–1383. Milkie, M.A., Mattingly, M.J., Nomaguchi, K.M., Bianchi, S.M., & Robinson, J.P. (2004). The time squeeze: Parental statuses and feelings about time with children. *Journal of Marriage and Family, 66*(3), 739–761.

23 Patterson, R. (2017). Could trends in time children spend with parents help explain the black–white gap in human capital? Evidence from the American Time Use Survey. *Education Economics, 25*(3), 219–233.

24 Todd, P.E., & Wolpin, K.I. (2007). The production of cognitive achievement in children: Home, school, and racial test score gaps. *Journal of Human Capital, 1*(1), 91–136.

25 Brooks-Gunn & Markman (2005).

26 Pridham, K., Denney, N., Pascoe, J., Chiu, Y., & Creasey, D. (1995). Mother's solutions to childbearing problems: Conditions and processes. *Journal of Marriage and the Family, 57*, 785–799.

27 Kalil, Ryan & Corey (2012).

28 Yamamoto & Sonnenschein (2016).

29 Guo & Harris (2000).

30 Nielsen, E.R. (2017). Human capital and wealth before and after capital in the 21st century. In H. Boushey, J.B. Delong, & M. Steinbaum (Eds.), *After Piketty: The Agenda for Economics and Inequality.* Cambridge, MA: Harvard University Press, pp. 150–169, p. 161.

31 Ermisch (2008).

32 Ibid., p. 68.

33 McLoyd, V.C. (1998). Socioeconomic disadvantage and child development. *American Psychologist, 53*(2), 185–204, p. 185.

34 Zimmermann, K.F., & Vogler, M. (Eds.). (2012). *Family, Household and Work.* Springer Science and Business Media.

35 Ibid., p. 218.

9 What are the implications for policy?

The different interpretations described above have important implications for policy. If poverty in itself restricts parental quality, the logical conclusion is that policy should relieve poverty. That is, policies should target poor families with income subsidies and tax relief. An emphasis should be given to support during the early years of a child's life. Such policies may also be easier to implement than those that seek to change family characteristics.[1]

However, if it is not poverty itself but parental behaviours that determine the skills and earning potential of their children, such policies will not change those behaviours. In which case it is likely that poverty will continue into the next generation, particularly if culture is still influencing parental behaviour. With this in mind, we must reconsider Guo and Harris's research.[2] If more money is redistributed to lower-income families, can we be assured that this will result in more cognitive stimulation and a change in parenting style?

If money is redistributed to those in lower socio-economic-situations, it may improve aspects of their lives, but there is no guarantee that money will be spent on educational resources nor that the parents will spend more time with their children. It does not ensure that problem resolution and communication strategies change, nor that children are given more structure. In which case, redistributing incomes is unlikely to target behaviours important for ending the cycles of inter-generational poverty.

If policies can enhance the capacity of parents to support their children's development, regardless of their socio-economic circumstances, it would take an important step in breaking the cycle of inter-generational poverty.[3] And enough evidence exists to show that effective parenting can protect children from many of the adverse effects of poverty.

However, at the present time, academics cannot say to what extent poverty can be mitigated by parental behaviour. More knowledge is needed on the mechanisms through which poverty influences parental behaviour. Nevertheless, there is evidence that effective parenting can buffer children from some of the adverse effects of socio-economic disadvantage and financial disadvantage.[4] This opens the exciting possibility that solution, or at least a partial solution exists for inter-generational poverty; that is the provision of parental programmes to improve parental skills.

A large body of research now exists showing that parenting is an important way to enhance child achievement at school entry.[5] This is the time when parents are the teachers, providing the cognitive scaffolding for later learning. The parental role is of prime importance because it occurs at an importance time in the child's development. The earliest years are when a child's cognitive skills are most malleable.[6]

Parental education has been defined as 'programs delivered in group settings, services and resources that provide parents and caregivers with specific knowledge and child-rearing skills that help foster children's development'.[7] Education programmes can provide parents with information on skills and practices that can improve their children's developmental outcomes.

Parental education programmes have emerged as a promising way of supporting parents and improving outcomes for children. Research to date shows that participation in such programmes 'has resulted in a number of benefits including reduced parental strength, increased parental self-efficacy, decreased use of harsh discipline, less difficulty addressing children's behaviour and improvement in children's problem behaviours'.[8]

And the benefit may be greatest for those who are most in need. For example, Finders et al. (2016) examined the effect of a programme on 2,344 parents in the Pacific North-West of the United States.[9] The research examined parent's perceptions of their own skills and children's behaviour having completed a programme. Results indicated a positive effect on both parents' self-reported skills and children's behaviours.

A significant body of work identifies the importance of the social transmission of knowledge from parent to child in the years before school.[10] The task is to identify what content should be on these programmes to improve parental practice. An earlier study by Hess and Holloway (1984) identified a number of features of effective parenting, including verbal interactions between mothers and children, parental expectations, positive affective relations, and discipline and control strategies.[11] More recent studies have confirmed the importance of emotional support and cognitive stimulation in the home environments.

One of the first areas for attention is the development of cognitive skills. Research shows that children whose parents engage in consistent home learning enter school with higher cognitive skills. These studies refer to both African American and Caucasian families and the results stand even in the presence of multiple risk factors.

Reading to children has long been known to be a positive parental practice. Duursma et al. (2008) found that frequent reading by the father to his children resulted in more advanced cognitive skills at the age of 36 months.[12] This finding was found to benefit low-income Hispanic families. Similarly, Baker (2013) found that parents who engaged in frequent home learning stimulation had children with more advanced reading and maths skills.[13] These results held after controlling for poverty. In other words:

> these studies suggest that fathers' and mothers' participation in home learning stimulation matters above and beyond demographic characteristics (e.g. poverty).[14]

A number of studies point to the importance of language proficiency. Liu et al. (2009) found that the children of Asian American mothers who were more proficient in English had better reading and maths scores.[15] Quiroz et al. (2010) found similar results for Hispanic families, where children of mothers with strong English proficiency had higher English vocabulary scores than those whose mothers had limited English.[16]

Baker (2016) found that language acculturation of Mexican Americans living in the United States predicted the reading and maths achievement of their children, after controlling for demographics.[17] It is argued that parents with stronger English-language skills are more likely to pass these skills along to their children. While acknowledging more research is needed, Baker also suggests that those with strong English skills may be more effective teachers of key cognitive skills needed on American standardised tests. The combined effect is a strengthening of the child's language and literacy skills.

Given the growing evidence that parent language acculturation matters for child achievement, Baker argued for language support programmes. Such programmes could provide resources and programmes which could

> be an opportunity for families and schools to collaborate and build lasting connections that will reinforce each other's commitment to improving children's early achievement and success.[18]

Language ability in early childhood is among the best predictors of later school success.[19] As early as school entry, many children from lower-socio-economic-status homes perform well below their peers on measures of language ability.[20] Vocabulary is important as it enhances a child's ability to express their feelings and desires. It also provides them with more conceptual tools to interpret and categorise the world around them.

A seminal paper in this area is that by Hart and Risley (1995) which estimated that 4-year-old children raised in poverty have heard 30 million words fewer than their more affluent peers.[21] Children in affluent families, have at the age of 3, produced double the words of children from low-income families. These early differences in exposure lead to gaps that remain stable or widen over time.[22] International studies reveal similar gaps. In a United Kingdom study of vocabulary, Blanden and Machin (2010) revealed that preschool children from low-income families were 15 months behind their more affluent peers,[23] while an Australian study showed an eight-month gap.[24]

Pace, Luo, Hirsh-Pasek and Golinkoff (2017) also focused on language development.[25] They considered three pathways by which socio-economic status influences verbal ability, and by targeting these pathways, their paper offers some hope for intervention. Focusing on the quantity and quality of parent–child interaction, they note a number of interventions that have been trialled with the goal of 'educating caregivers on the importance of early language input and improving the quality and quantity of language and literacy interactions'.[26]

These interventions have shown notable success. They cited the Thirty Million Words Initiative[27] which instructs parents to talk more and provides parents with feedback on their language. This programme successfully increased the number of words used in parent–child interactions at home.[28] Another positive intervention in the United Kingdom encouraged parents to engage in contingent talk with their infants for 15 minutes a day.[29] Another successful intervention encouraged caregivers to engage in shared book-reading and joint writing several times a week.[30] Some interventions focused more broadly on the quality of parenting practices, training low-income mothers to respond to their children with warmth, sensitivity and in a contingent manner.[31]

A common theme of these interventions is that language skills are malleable, and can be improved regardless of the income of the parents. Nevertheless, one of the pathways identified by Pace et al. (2017) is the number of learning resources available.[32] Low SES families have fewer, if any, learning resources. An effective strategy to overcome this is through the provision of easier access to literacy materials. In particular, interventions that encourage full use of libraries.

It is not just educational activities that influences a child's development. Research also highlights the importance of a broader range of parenting activities, including the development of self-discipline, socialisation, attentional control, and emotional regulation.[33] Hence, it is important to consider not just cognitive skills but also non-cognitive skills.

Providing structure is important. Parental practices that contribute to this include the establishment of regular times for family meals, rules for using computers and television, as well as routines for bedtime and homework. Such structure has been linked to positive health and developmental outcomes for children.[34]

Another capability that has been linked to success in the modern economy is social skills.[35] Developmental psychologists have conducted research into the development of social competence which has been defined as a child's ability to 'form close and secure adult and peer relationships; experience, regulate, and express emotions in socially and culturally appropriate ways; and explore the environment and learn'.[36]

An extensive body of research has revealed the importance that interaction with primary caregivers has on the development of a child's social competence.[37] For example, Foster et al. studied the effect of joint activities, focusing on literacy in 48 Head Start classrooms in the United States.[38] They found a significant relationship between children's participation in home learning activities and their social functioning. Of equal importance was the finding that this effect also mediated the relationship between socio-economic status (SES) and school outcomes.

A key element of parenting styles is the way that parents deal with conflict. Instead of using punitive measures, reasoning with the child and explaining the logic of rules is seen as far more effective, and is associated with good emotional balance, capacity for self-regulation, good self-esteem, the ability to understand another person's point of view.[39] This, in turn, is associated with better social relations later in life and greater social maturity.

A childhood capability with a strong link to socio-economic outcomes is self-control. An early study in this area was the famed marshmallow test conducted by Stanford psychologist Walter Mischel.[40] In this study, preschool children were presented with a marshmallow. The children were then told that the experimenter would leave the room and they could eat the marshmallow in the experimenter's absence. However, if they waited until the experimenter returned, they would get a second marshmallow. There was significant variation in how long the children could put off eating the marshmallow in front of them.

Mischel's study did not end there. His daughters attended the same school as children in the test, and he would occasionally ask them how the children were progressing through school. A pattern appeared in which those who showed the most self-control were the ones doing best at school. This encouraged him to track their progress and he discovered that those who showed the most self-control at the age of 4–5 had higher SAT scores in high school, showed greater social skills and resilience as adolescents. These benefits continued as the children aged.

The benefits of self-control have been observed in a number of studies. A longitudinal study conducted by Moffitt et al. (2013) assessed the effect of self-control on socio-economic outcomes.[41] This was a 40-year study drawing on over 1,000 children born in 1972 and 1973. Each child's self-control was assessed through a number of measures at the ages 3, 5, 7, 9 and 11. Comparisons were made with their socio-economic outcomes later in life. The study found that poor self-control in childhood foreshadowed poor outcomes in adulthood.

People who exhibited poor self-control in their childhood experienced a number of problems in their 30s. They were more likely to experience problems such as low income, poor saving habits, credit problems, and social welfare dependence. They were also more prone to health problems and crime. Significantly, children with poor self-control were likely to perform poorly in school and the income earned later in life.[42]

Moffitt and her colleagues came to the conclusion that self-control skills are so important that, if they can be taught, they would benefit all children regardless of their background and intelligence.[43] Fortunately, evidence suggests that such capabilities can be taught.[44] Programmes that enhance children's self-control include martial arts, music lessons, some computer games, mastering a second language. Notably, some programmes have targeted parents with coaching on how to raise their child's self-control.[45]

A related concept is self-regulation. Self-regulation has been defined as a multidimensional construct that includes the regulation of emotions, behaviours and cognitions.[46] A body of research has revealed that low-income Mexican American children are prone to having low self-regulation.[47] A study by Díaz and McClelland (2017) revealed that parental control had a significant positive relation to children's self-regulation.[48] It was previously believed that high levels of parental control denied children the chance to practice their own self-regulation skills. However, this research suggests that might not be the case.[49] This is consistent with Asian parenting where a high level of control helps to set clear behavioural expectations for children. The authors of this study conclude that 'to promote self-regulation skills in low-income Mexican American children, it is essential to understand the influence of parenting practices ...', as well as the conventional explanations.[50]

These studies suggest that parental programmes could enhance a number of areas of development that impact on a child's future welfare. These include cognitive stimulation, language and vocabulary, self-control and social skills, and the provision of structure. In confirming the importance of children's home experiences for their early academic development, studies like these offer exciting hope that interventions can be created that reduce the ethnic wealth and academic gap. by fostering awareness in parents of what they can do to facilitate their children's growth.

Notes

1 McLoyd (1998).
2 Guo & Harris (2000).
3 Cobb-Clark, D.A., Salamanca, N., & Zhu, A. (2016). *Parenting Style as an Investment in Human Development* (February 8). Melbourne Institute Working Paper No. 3/16. Available at SSRN: https://ssrn.com/abstract=2729578 or http://dx.doi.org/10.2139/ssrn.2729578.
4 McLoyd (1998); Guo, & Harris (2000); McCulloch, A., & Joshi, H.E. (2002). Child development and family resources: Evidence from the second generation of the 1958 British birth cohort. *Journal of Population Economics, 15*(2), 283–304.
5 Baker, C.E., Cameron, C.E., Rimm-Kaufman, S.E., et al. (2012). Family and socio-demographic predictors of school readiness among African American boys in kindergarten. *Early Education and Development, 23*, 833–854; Baker, C.E., & Iruka, I.U. (2013). Maternal psychological functioning and children's school readiness: The mediating role of home environments for African American children. *Early Childhood Research Quarterly, 28*, 509–519; Burchinal, M., Vernon-Feagans, L., & Cox, M. (2008). Cumulative social risk, parenting, and infant development in rural low-income communities. *Parenting: Science and Practice, 8*, 41–69. Cabrera, N.J., Beeghly, M., & Eisenberg, N. (2012). Positive development of minority children: Introduction to the special issue. *Child Development Perspectives, 6*, 207–209.
6 Cunha, F., Heckman, J., & Schennach, S. (2010). Estimating the technology of cognitive and non-cognitive skill formation. *Econometrica: Journal of the Econometric Society, 78*(3), 883–931.
7 Zepeda, M., Varela, F., & Morales, A. (2004). *Promoting Positive Parenting Practices through Parenting Education: Building State Early Childhood Comprehensive Systems Series*, Number 13. UCLA Center for Healthier Children, Families and Communities.
8 Finders, J.K., Díaz, G., Geldhof, G.J., Sektnan, M., & Rennekamp. D. (2016). The impact of parenting education on parent and child behaviors: Moderators by income and ethnicity. *Children and Youth Services Review, 71*, 199–209.
9 Ibid.
10 Baker, C.E. (2016). Fathers' and mothers' language acculturation and parenting practices: Links to Mexican American children's academic readiness. *Journal of Early Childhood Research*, 1476718X15614044. Baker, C.E., & Rimm-Kaufman, S.E. (2014). How home influence schools: Early parenting predicts African American children's classroom social emotional functioning. *Psychology in the Schools, 51*, 722–735. Bronfenbrenner, U., & Morris, P.A. (1998) The ecology of developmental processes. In R. Lerner (Ed.), *Handbook of Child Psychology*, vol. 1. New York: Wiley, pp. 993–1028. Baker, C.E.,

Vernon-Feagans, L., The Family Life Project Investigators (2015). Fathers' language input during shared book activities: Links to children's kindergarten achievement. *Journal of Applied Developmental Psychology, 36*, 53–59; Burchinal et al. (2008).

11 Hess, R., & Holloway, S. (1984). Family and school as educational institutions. In R. D. Parke (Ed.), *Review of Child Development Research*, Vol. 7. Chicago: University of Chicago Press, pp. 179–22.

12 Duursma, E., Pan, B.A., & Raikes, H. (2008). Predictors and outcomes of low-income fathers' reading with their toddlers. *Early Childhood Research Quarterly*, 23, 351–365.

13 Baker, C.E. (2013). Fathers' and mothers' home literacy involvement and children's cognitive and social emotional development: Implications for family literacy programs. *Applied Developmental Science, 17*, 184–197.

14 Baker (2016), p. 55.

15 Liu, L.K., Benner A.D., & Lau A.S. (2009). Mother-adolescent language proficiency and adolescent academic and emotional adjustment among Chinese American families. *Journal of Youth and Adolescence, 38*, 572–586.

16 Quiroz, B.G., Snow, C.E., & Zhao, J. (2010). Vocabulary skills of Spanish–English bilinguals: Impact of mother–child language interactions and home language and literacy support. *International Journal of Bilingualism, 14*, 379–399.

17 Baker (2016).

18 Ibid., p. 6 2.

19 Burchinal, M.R., Pace, A., Alper, R., Hirsh-Pasek, K., & Golinkoff, R.M. (2016). *Early Language Outshines Other Predictors of Academic and Social Trajectories in Elementary School.* Presented at Assoc. Child. Fam. Conf. (ACF), Washington, DC, July 11–13; Hoff, E. (2013). Interpreting the early language trajectories of children from low-SES and language minority homes: Implications for closing achievement gaps. *Developmental Psychology, 49*, 4–14.

20 Ginsborg, J. (2006). The effects of socio-economic status on children's language acquisition and use. In J. Clegg & J. Ginsborg (Eds.) *Language and Social Disadvantage: Theory into Practice.* Hoboken, NJ: Wiley, pp. 9–27.

21 Hart, B., & Risley, T.R. (1995). *Meaningful Differences in the Everyday Experience of Young American Children.* Baltimore, MD: Paul H. Brookes.

22 Walker, D., Greenwood, C., Hart, B., & Carta, J. (1994). Prediction of school outcomes based on early language production and socioeconomic factors. *Child Development, 65*, 606–621. Fernald, A., Marchman, V., & Weisleder, A. (2013). SES differences in language processing skill and vocabulary are evident at 18 months. *Development Science, 16*, 234–248.

23 Blanden, J., & Machin, S. (2010). Intergenerational inequality in early years assessments. In K. Hansen, H. Joshi, & S. Dex (Eds.), *Children of the 21st Century: The First Five Years.* London: Centre of Longitudinal Studies, pp. 153–168.

24 Taylor, C.L., Christensen, D., Lawrence, D., Mitrou, F., & Zubrick, S.R. (2013). Risk factors for children's receptive vocabulary development from four to eight years in the longitudinal study of Australian children. *PLOS ONE* 8:e73046.

25 Pace, A., Luo, R., Hirsh-Pasek, K., & Golinkoff, R.M. (2017). Identifying pathways between socioeconomic status and language development. *Annual Review of Linguistics, 3*, 285–308.

26 Ibid., p. 297.

27 http://thirtymillionwords.org/.

28 Suskind, D., Leffel, K.R., Hernandez, M.W., Sapolich, S.G., Suskind, E., et al. (2013). An exploratory study of 'quantitative linguistic feedback': Effect of LENA feedback on adult language production. *Communication Disorders Quarterly, 34*, 199–209.

29 McGillion, M., Herbert, J., Pine, J., & Matthews. D. (2014). *The Relation between Caregiver Contingent Talk, SES and Language Learning: An Intervention Study.* Presented at 14th International Conference Infant Studies, Berlin.

30 Levin, I., & Aram, D. (2012). Mother–child joint writing and storybook reading and their effects on kindergartners' literacy: An intervention study. *Reading and Writing, 25*, 217–249.
31 Landry, S.H., Smith, K.E., & Swank, P.R. (2006). Responsive parenting: Establishing early foundations for social, communication, and independent problem-solving skills. *Developmental Psychology, 42*, 627–642; Landry, S.H., Smith, K.E., Swank, P.R., & Guttentag, C. (2008). A responsive parenting intervention: The optimal timing across early childhood for impacting maternal behaviors and child outcomes. *Developmental Psychology, 44*, 1335–1353.
32 Pace et al. (2017).
33 Borghans, L., Meijers, H., & Ter Weel, B. (2008). The role of non-cognitive skills in explaining cognitive test scores. *Economic Inquiry, 46*(1), 2–12.
34 Del Bono, E., Francesconi, M., Kelly, Y., & Sacker, A. (2014). *Early Maternal Time Investment and Early Child Outcomes.* University of Essex Department of Economics Discussion Paper Series, No. 726; Ribar, D.C., & Zapata, D. (2014). Food assistance and family routines in three American cities. *Review of Economics of the Household, 10*, 1–16.
35 Clydesdale, G. (2013) *Human Nature: A Guide to Managing Workplace Relations.* Farnham: Gower.
36 Yates, T., Ostrosky, M.M., Cheatham, G.A., Fettig, A., Shaffer, L., & Santos, R.M. (2008). Research synthesis on screening and assessing social-emotional competence. The Center on the Social and Emotional Foundations of Learning (CSEFL). Retrieved 25 April 2015, from http://csefel.vanderbilt.edu/documents/rs_screening_assessment.pdf, p. 2.
37 Gadaire, D.M., Henrich, C.C., & Finn-Stevenson, M. (2016). Longitudinal effects of parent–child interactions on children's social competence. *Research on Social Work Practice, 27*(7), 767–778; Foster, M.A., Lambert, R., Abbott-Shim, M., McCarty, F., & Franze, S. (2005). A model of home learning environment and social risk factors in relation to literacy and social outcomes. *Early Childhood Research Quarterly, 20*, 13–36; McCart, M. R., Priester, P.E., Davies, W.H., & Azen, R. (2006). Differential effectiveness of behavioral parent-training and cognitive-behavioral therapy for antisocial youth: A meta-analysis. *Journal of Abnormal Child Psychology, 34*, 525–541.
38 Foster, Lambert, Abbott-Shim, McCarty & Franze (2005).
39 Freijo (2005).
40 Mischel, W., Ebbesen, E.B., & Raskoff Zeiss, A. (1972). Cognitive and attentional mechanisms in delay of gratification. *Journal of Personality and Social Psychology, 21*(2), 204–218; Mischel, W. (2014). *The Marshmallow Test: Understanding Self-control and How to Master It.* London: Random House.
41 Moffitt, T.E., Poulton, R., & Caspi, A. (2013). Lifelong impact of early self-control. *American Scientist, 101*, 352.
42 Moffitt, T.E., Arseneault, L., Belsky, D., Dickson, N., Hancox, R.J., Harrington, H., Houts, R., Poulton, R., Roberts, B., Ross, S., Thompson, W.M., Caspi, A., & Sears, M. R. (2011). A gradient of childhood self-control predicts health, wealth, and public safety. *Proceedings of the National Academy of Sciences, 108*, 2693–2698.
43 Moffitt et al. (2013).
44 Roberts, B.W., Walton, K.E., & Viechtbauer, W. (2006). Patterns of mean-level change in personality traits across the life course: A meta-analysis of longitudinal studies. *Psychological Bulletin, 132*, 1.
45 Moffitt et al. (2013).
46 Díaz, G., & McClelland, M.M. (2017). The influence of parenting on Mexican American children's self-regulation. *PsyCh Journal, 6*(1), 43–56.
47 Galindo, C., & Fuller, B. (2010). The social competence of Latino kindergartners and growth in mathematical understanding. *Developmental Psychology, 46*(3), 579–592. Wanless, S.B., McClelland, M.M., Tominey, S.L., & Acock, A.C. (2011). The influence

of demographic risk factors on children's behavioral regulation in prekindergarten and kindergarten. *Early Education & Development, 22*(3), 461–488.

48 Díaz & McClelland (2017).

49 Grolnick, W.S., & Ryan, R.M. (1989). Parent styles associated with children's self-regulation and competence in school. *Journal of Educational Psychology, 81*, 143–154; Kochanska, G., & Knaack, A. (2003). Effortful control as a personality characteristic of young children: Antecedents, correlates, and consequences. *Journal of Personality*, 71, 1087–1112.

50 Díaz & McClelland (2017).

10 Two case studies

Maori poverty

Maori and Pacific people both experience a lower socio-economic position in New Zealand society; however, there are big differences in the path they took to their current situation. Maori were colonised by British imperialists in the early nineteenth century. By contrast, Polynesians migrated to New Zealand in the late twentieth century. It could be argued that Polynesians were colonised in their own islands prior to their immigration. However, in most cases they maintained their traditional land and tribal structures. It was in New Zealand where they encountered significant socio-economic change.

Maori, by contrast, did not choose to migrate, but had a new socio-economic system placed upon them. The colonial trauma argument has been used to explain their position but it cannot be used to describe the Polynesian situation. Another explanation might be discrimination; however, surveys of Pacific immigrants reveal high levels of satisfaction with their life in New Zealand and continually choose to emigrate there.

Although their two recent histories are different, they nevertheless share four common features. First, they both experience low socio-economic status. Second, they have both experienced socio-economic change and third, they both have poor academic outcomes compared to other ethnic groups.

The fourth commonality refers to their traditional cultures. Before colonisation, both were located in the South Pacific, isolated from the knowledge and commercial advances that flowed across the Eurasian continent. This isolation meant they would never have the opportunity to hear of Chinese advances in printing, the Hindu-Arabic numeral system, or Newtonian physics. Their economy and culture were based on localised resources and knowledge.

For Maori, the first ongoing interaction with global economic and knowledge flows occurred in 1776 when the British explorer James Cook arrived in New Zealand. At that time, the Enlightenment and industrial revolution were underway in Europe. Britain was not yet a knowledge economy but it was increasingly developing knowledge with the purpose of advancing welfare. By contrast, both Maori and Pacific Islanders had no literature, science or maths. By the mid-nineteenth century, when Europeans were making huge advances in literacy, book publishing, science, commerce and industry, Maori were just beginning to read.

Probably the earliest description of Maori parenting practices and education comes from a Maori woman named Anahe who became a lover to a sailor from Captain Cook's ship the *Resolution* which visited New Zealand in 1777. Anahe gave her lover much information on Maori life and customs including the following:

> the fathers had sole care of the boys as soon as they could walk, and that the girls were left wholly at the mother's disposal. She said it was a crime for a mother to correct her son after he was once taken under the protection of the father; and that it was always resented by the mother if the father interfered in the management of the daughters. She said, the boys from their infancy were trained to war, and both boys and girls were taught the art of fishing, to weave their nets, and make their hooks and lines; that their canoes came from a far country, and that they got them in exchange for cloth which was chiefly manufactured by the women …[1]

An interesting aspect of this comment is that trade was practised and the women were taught to make things for exchange. However, trade was limited as this was predominantly a subsistence economy. Hence, a child's education was devoted to the skills needed, including preparedness for war.

For six decades after Cook's arrival in NZ, Maori interaction with Europe was small-scale and the traditional socio-economic system predominated. But influences from the West were encroaching. Missionaries introduced new beliefs and the beginnings of formal schooling. New products and crops helped enhance welfare. However, the introduction of the musket escalated traditional tribal rivalries and reduced welfare for many.

Maori were about to endure significant changes in their resource base and economic system. One of the things that excited Maori most about their initial interactions with Europeans was the possibility of trade and being part of a global economy which brought many life-enhancing goods. However, trade in Maori society was done on a small scale, and the transition to a predominantly market economy would lead to significant demands on their own socio-economic structure and parental practices.

The pace of colonisation increased after 1840 and the extent that the Maori economy changed in these years is significant. Bedggood (1978) took a Marxist view of the situation and noted that colonisation involved the replacement of indigenous economic structures with capitalist structures. He notes that 'the penetration of the capitalist mode of production and the destruction of the Maori occurred at three levels, economic, political and legal'.[2]

The problem for Maori was their economic system and skill-base was so different to that in the West. Europeans and the countries populated by their descendants were enjoying first mover advantages in the development of a knowledge economy. Maori and other Pacific people had not even begun. Seen in this light, their material position could be interpreted as a process of catch-up. That is not to say that Maori lacked skills. On the contrary. The Maori economic system required its members to attain a high level of skills, but different skills to those being built by Europeans.

No one lacked faith in the potential of Maori, nor their intellectual capacity. Europeans regularly commented on the intelligence of Maori and their potential. As the Reverend Samuel Marsden noted 'a finer race of men has seldom, if ever been found in any country'.[3] In many capabilities, they surpassed Europeans, a reflection of what their culture nurtured. The ethnographer Elsdon Best recognised a number of these. He noted that their ...

> ability in hand to hand combats was remarkable, the result of continued training from boyhood. In marching with heavy packs, lifting weights, and other such tests they are superior to the average European ... (Similarly) In the senses of sight and hearing, the Maori has a marked advantage over us.[4]

They also had strong capabilities in some cognitive skills. Best notes:

> The Maori is mentally acute and possesses remarkable powers of comprehension. His powers of memory are undoubtedly great and sometimes appear marvellous to us. Thus, an old man of the Tuhoe tribe recited to the writer no less than 406 songs from memory. Another old fellow recited from memory the genealogy of his clan, a task that necessitated the repetition of over 1,400 personal names. Such powers of memorising are the result of long centuries of training, of the lack of a written tongue, combined with a strong desire to perpetuate certain forms of knowledge.[5]

Once again, this capability appears to be linked to child-rearing. As babies, parents would sing lullabies to their children which included the child's genealogy (whakapapa). These lullabies were composed and sung to the babies as a socialising skill to mould the child as a useful member of the tribe. They were sung repeatedly to fix personal, family and cultural messages in the minds of the listeners.[6] Songs were also sung to motivate children towards desired behaviours.

Education continued as they grew. Jenkins and Harte (2011) note that a Maori child's 'whole life was training. Everything they saw and did prepared them for adulthood. Children, boys and girls, had to be prepared for life as warriors, food producers, parents and marital partners.'[7]

A key feature of the Maori economy was the need to gain resources from hunting. Hence, they developed an ability to track and find prey. Europeans were impressed by their abilities, as one noted:

> It's amazing how acute senses these Nations have ... the Natives often shewed Me Ducks or Snipes or other birds, where none of us could distinguish any.[8]

The idea that a culture embeds its members with specific skills and abilities is important to understanding some forms of poverty. Maori excelled in hunting and two hundred years later at the end of the twentieth century, many white New Zealanders would state that rural Maori maintained their prowess.

While Maori were certainly superior to the Europeans in this ability, they had not developed capabilities for farming animals. When early Europeans left a sow and boar in New Zealand to mate and provide the basis of an enduring supply of meat, the Maori divided the pigs between themselves. This meant that the pigs could not breed, and led one observer to make the following uncomplimentary comment:

> Thus, by separating the animals, and dividing them as spoil, these barbarians effectually destroy the possibility of propagating the species. Too preoccupied with the wants of the present moment, they overlook the only means of securing a certain livelihood to themselves and reject every attempt to civilise them.[9]

The Maori tendency for immediate consumption may reflect a pattern of behaviour identified by Barry, Child and Bacon (1959) who noted that in economies based on hunting and gathering, their food was immediately consumed.[10] By contrast, in economies based on agriculture, consumption was less immediate. These differences translated into different parental behaviour. Societies that accumulated food over time needed adults who were responsible, conservative and respectful of elders. Hence, in agricultural cultures, children were brought up with a strong emphasis on obedience and responsibility. By contrast, cultures like Maori encouraged their children towards achievement, self-reliance and independence. This difference should not be over-stated as some tribes did have extensive crops and storage pits. Nevertheless, there was substantial difference between Europeans and Maori in food attainment.

This pattern is supported by descriptions of Maori parenting which reveal that there was little emphasis on self-discipline and constraint. As the anthropologist Firth noted:

> The discipline was slight, as it was thought desirable that the child should preserve its spirit unbroken, proud and fierce, the better to be able to cope with the difficulties of later life.[11]

These characteristics of low discipline and immediate consumption may have implications carried forward as self-regulation/control has been identified as important for success in the modern economy. This lack of discipline may also have had an effect on employment practices well into the twentieth century. Trainers had trouble dealing with the Maori free spirit, as one trainer of farm cadets noted:

> Always restless under apprenticeship. and anxious to make big wages on labouring jobs … the young Maoris, as young Maoris are inclined to do, drifted away from their employment.[12]

This attitude may also reflect the fact that the whole idea of working for another person was a totally new concept. Maori had made some goods for market exchange, but the idea of a labour market was foreign. Theirs was predominantly a subsistence economy and the idea of selling their labour for exchange was not practised. The idea of training for a labour market and the unique demands of employment was completely foreign. It required a sense of time discipline and although, like all peoples, they had a sense of seasons and changes throughout the day, the notion of working to a clock was never part of their culture. In fact, the whole idea of clocks and watches was new. Hence, one observer noted that 'Time was not at all precious to the Maori.'[13]

One area in which Maori had a particular disadvantage was in academic socialisation. This was a society devoid of science, literature and formal mathematics education. However, from the outset, mission schools sought to remedy this and Maori were keen to acquire these new skills. One who observed this first hand was Lady Martin who noted that 'The children were eager to be taught.' They 'are pleasant to teach, they are so wide-awake and full of fun.' This keenness also extended to adults and she noted 'how readily the adult Maoris teach themselves to write'.[14]

Sadly, one of the worst colonial government decisions occurred with the Native Schools Act of 1867 which prohibited the use of Maori at school. Maori were disciplined if they spoke in their own language. Such actions would not incline Maori towards contemporary education.

Over time, it became apparent that Maori were struggling in the new economic system. Maori were caught in a cultural mis-match. Europeans were arriving with new products and new production methods. The old productive methods of Maori were not as effective as those from Europe, so were discarded. However, Maori were not as proficient with the new methods as the white settlers. They were engaged in a process of catch-up with a people that were continuing to move ahead. A government report noted:

> They have lost the habits of industry of their ancestors, and they have not acquired the habits of the European in this respect … The spectacle is presented to us of a people starving in the midst of plenty.[15]

The government was well aware that Maori were undergoing a transition process which their culture had not prepared them for. In 1891, Sir Robert Stout noted that

> The natives cannot equal the Europeans in buying, or selling, or in other things. They have not gone through the long process of evolution which the white race has gone through.[16]

James Carroll, who was a member of the Native Land Laws Commission made similar comments:

> no attempt has been made to educate them in acquiring industrial knowledge or … industrial pursuits.[17]

In 1907, a commission looked at the issue in depth. This commission is notable for the fact that one of Maori's most distinguished leaders, Apirana Ngata was one of the authors:

> If the Maori is to become an industrious citizen steps will have to be taken to provide for his education different from the steps that have been taken in the past. He may in our opinion become an efficient settler – just as efficient as the European settler. But it cannot be expected that he can equal a race that has been farming for thousands of years, whilst his race has only been engaged in what may be termed hunting and in the culture of small garden patches.[18]

This Commission recommended that the government establish training programmes where selected Maori youths may be taught modern agricultural technique. When Apirana Ngata became Native Minister in 1928, he continued this emphasis on building modern capabilities with a number of programmes. Today, he is widely acknowledged for his work in this area.

These policies worked. By 1951, 90% of Maori were recorded as wage earners. Maori children received education in primary and secondary schools and many young men had acquired skills in trades and professions. This led to a 'striking improvement in the economic position of Maori people'.[19]

However, disparities remained. Maori continued to perform poorly on a wide range of socio-economic indicators including health, unemployment, crime, home ownership incomes and educational outcomes.[20] As Maori became more aware of their position, the explanation for their status changed from 'catch-up' to cultural trauma and discrimination.

There was certainly evidence of discrimination and poor government policy to back these claims. Standing out is the aforementioned Native Schools Act 1867, which prohibited the use of the Maori language at school. Equally destructive was the confiscation of a significant amount of land that reduced the asset base of Maori tribes.

Maori lost ownership of huge tracts of land after the arrival of Europeans. Much of this land was sold by Maori and it has been argued that Maori were not aware that they were losing the land for good when they sold. They merely thought they were giving temporary property rights away, not ownership. To make matters worse, many European buyers did not fulfil the obligations of their purchase agreements.

The government participated in this land-loss in the 1860s when wars erupted which gave the colonial government opportunity to confiscate land from the belligerents. A Native Land Court was established to settle claims of ownership but it favoured European settlers over Maori and any surplus land was kept by the crown and not returned to their Maori owners.

Much of what is described today as colonial trauma has been linked to this land-loss. Loss of such an asset must have impacted on their wealth and future earning potential. However, there are limits to this argument. First, Maori still retained a huge land-base. At the end of the nineteenth century, when disparities in wealth had become significant, Maori owned one-sixth of the country even though they only constituted one-fifteenth of the population.[21] As a race they were rich in land, and much of it was fertile.

Second, not all of the tribes lost land. In fact, those that kept their land rank among the poorest today. These are areas where the Maori population is high, and traditional behaviours have not been 'saturated' by Western methods as deeply as those in the cities.

Cultural trauma may have occurred with Maori but these facts raise serious questions over whether this explains Maori poverty. There is no doubt that injustices occurred which would have impacted on wealth and income, but if pushed too far, the explanation blurs the path to developing effective solutions.

The cultural trauma argument may also be unfair on the colonisers. Maori did not experience the genocide and extermination of Native Americans. In fact, Maori experiences of genocide came before colonisation with warriors such as Te Rauparaha who sought to exterminate enemy tribes. Nor did they experience slavery. In fact, their own indigenous practices allowed slavery which was practised on a wide scale before colonisation. Yet none of the analyses of trauma on New Zealand Maori suggest that these indigenous practices had an effect as great as colonisation. It is ironic that these practices with a strong association with colonial trauma were actually put to an end by the British.

Policies with a focus on parenting and academic socialisation may have other significant benefits for Maori. Today, Maori remain disproportionately represented in prison. Fifty-one percent of the offender population is Maori despite only representing 15.8% of the general population.[22] The figure for women is even worse, at 63% of the female prison population. A related figure is the number of Maori children who are reported to government agencies. Maori make up 57% of children referred to the Department for Child, Youth and Families, and it is recognised that those children who have been under the state care and protection system are more likely to end up in jail as an adult.[23]

There is a strong link to academic achievement and prison. Department of Correction figures indicate that 65% of people in prison require literacy support.[24] They are functionally illiterate. Hence, the Department is increasing emphasis on both educational services and parental skills. For example, in reference to a prison based 'bedtime stories' programme in which female prisoners read stories to their children, the Department state:

> Improved literacy has benefits for families as well as the women themselves.[25]

In the meantime, the labour market continues to evolve and favour those people with the highest academic outcomes. It continues to favour those with capabilities in mathematics, science and the ability to read and write. Maori did not possess these capabilities until the mid-nineteenth century and statistics on education suggest that Maori still have a significant disadvantage in these most important of areas. Seen in this light, the old explanation of catch-up as argued by Apirana Ngata and his colleagues, needs to be re-visited and deepened to the base of human capital development; parenting.

Pacific poverty in New Zealand

Another ethnic minority in New Zealand to feature at the lower end of the socio-economic spectrum are the Pacific peoples, often referred to as Pasifika or Polynesians. It includes Samoans, Tongans, Tokelauans, Cook Islanders and Niueans. Like Maori, these people were historically cut off from the knowledge and technological advances that flowed across the Eurasian continent by the Pacific Ocean.

Unlike Maori who had cultural change brought upon them, Pacific people chose to migrate to New Zealand and its different culture. The first major flows of Pacific migrants began in the 1950s and 1960s. By the mid-1970s, academics noted that these people were emerging into an underclass. For example, MacPherson (1977) used the term 'eth-class; a situation in which minority ethnicity and lower socio-economic status coincide and are likely to do so permanently'.[26] He noted:

> on all the conventional indicators of socio-economic status the Polynesian minorities can be seen to be lower overall than their European counterparts. The Polynesian has achieved less from education than his European counterparts, he has taken a disproportionately large share of the unskilled and semi-skilled jobs and as a consequence earns less than his European counterpart.[27]

A generation later, the problem remained. MacPherson and other sociologists repeated the claims noting 'the sorry statistical picture which was given of a marginalised minority in New Zealand society – an "underclass" with some inter-generational dimensions of deprivation and disadvantage'.[28]

Policies were introduced to address this situation but 13 years later, the same observations remain. Perry (2013) noted that poverty rates for 'Pacific ethnic groups are consistently higher than for those in the European/Pakeha ethnic group (roughly double), whatever measure is used.'[29]

Decades of government policy have failed to address this situation. In fact, New Zealand has seen a dramatic rise in Pacific people living on the lowest income levels. It has risen from 13% in 1982 to 22% in 2013. In this time, the Pacific population in New Zealand had grown from approximately 120,000 to approximately 295,944.[30] This data tells us that the number of Pacific people living on low incomes in New Zealand has risen from approximately 15,600 to 65,107. The persistence of this problem raises many questions including what is its cause and why has government failed to solve it. McNaughton and Lai (2008) stated:

> New Zealand researchers and policy makers have known for some time that we have not served these communities as well as others.[31]

In this section, we will examine the policies used to fight Pacific poverty and the reason for their failure. Past policies have focused on income redistribution and incorporating diverse Pacific cultures into New Zealand society. However, they have not produced the desired results and inter-generational poverty remains a concern to the government today.

By definition, income redistribution should be an effective weapon in fighting poverty; however, it has had limited effect. For example, in 2007, the Labour government introduced 'Working for Families', a distributional policy with great expectations. On its release, the Minister of Pacific Island Affairs stated:

> Working for Families is increasing the incomes of hundreds of thousands of New Zealand's working and beneficiary families, and lifting tens of thousands of children out of poverty ...[32]

The Minister stated that, with the introduction of this programme, most Pacific people in New Zealand paid no net tax.[33] The 'Working for Families' programme was a substantial investment in poverty[34] and significantly raised incomes for Pacific people. However, five years on, Pacific poverty rates had not improved. In fact, the income gap between Pacific people and the European majority had widened sharply.[35] Pacific incomes had actually fallen. Perry (2013) revealed that 22% of Pacific people are living in poverty with unemployment rates of 15.7% compared to 4.9% for Europeans.[36] After significant income redistribution and ten consecutive quarters of economic growth, 30% of Pacific children are still living on the poverty line.[37]

Income redistribution can be an effective tool in alleviating poverty, but if there is an underlying cause of poverty, income redistribution by itself may not change income generating behaviours. Pacific people will remain disproportionately employed in low-income positions, a reflection of their poor educational outcomes.

The Ministry charged with improving the livelihood of Pacific people is the Ministry of Pacific peoples. A recent review of the Ministry noted that it had failed to lift incomes and standards of living for Pacific people.[38] However, one of the few areas that the Ministry did perform well was 'promoting Pacific language and culture'. These two results are consistent with the policies used.

Together with the Ministry of Education, the Ministry has an emphasis on promoting multi-culturalism and getting teachers to respect the Pacific way.[39] This approach claimed that Pacific students require a different type of teaching. For example, it appears that Pacific students respond better to firm directions rather than being expected to be self-motivated.[40]

The logic of basing an education system on a migrant's home culture has some support. One successful programme for Maori was the development of 'language nests' (Kohanga Reo) which provided an introduction to early education but within the Maori language. This programme was started by Sir Peter Sharples with the prime goal of rejuvenating the Maori language. It succeeded but had one other benefit. It helped many Maori parents gain a stronger appreciation of education and helped raise education levels. In this sense, the policies argued in this book are an extension of this policy, that is to foster a strong education mentality in Maori and Pacific students.

The Kohanga Reo programme was an excellent intervention and may be transferable to other ethnic groups. However, there is also a key difference between

Pacific and Maori people, that is Pacific parents have always valued education much higher than Maori. A second concern is how far do you push 'cultural education' if the people themselves want the higher levels of wealth that come from a different culture. Of course, it is not an either/or question. It is more of a case of recognising what cultural components provide the wealth levels they seek.

Mila-Schaaf and Robinson (2010) argued that Pacific culture may be associated with enhanced educational outcomes. They noted that 'being proud of Pacific ethnic identity and placing importance on Pacific ethnic values was associated with being twice as likely to report doing well at school'.[41] This initially sounds encouraging; however, the measure of doing well is being either 'about the middle' or 'above the middle' of a low-performing school.

Much of the policy has devoted resources to maintaining Pacific languages, and international evidence exists to support such a policy. For example, Portes and Schauffler (1994) studied immigrants to the USA and found bilingual migrant children performed better on a number of academic measures than those who had not retained their language of origin.[42] These claims are supported by Garcia (2003) and Sweet and Snow (2003) who reveal that children with English as a second language can transfer their first-language skills and actually enhance their learning of English.[43] It is also argued that language and culture of origin can also help learning by raising self-esteem, identity and confidence. The student's prior knowledge can be used as a foundation for scaffolding their learning.[44] It also helps to avoid language barriers, including unfamiliar concepts and words that relate to things that the students had not experienced or have equivalent translations for.

Some New Zealand studies have supported this line of thinking. For example, Amituanai-Toloa and McNaughton (2008) found that Samoan primary school students who are instructed in both Samoan and English achieved higher academic scores than those who were instructed only in English.[45] However, in a more recent study, the results were mixed.[46]

In New Zealand, there is a 'general consensus' that school children who have English as a second language (such as Pacific children) but who are adept in their first language can transfer their language skills to enhance their English competence.[47] One writer believes the link is so strong that the decline in speaking their first language can have negative implications for their general education. In fact, when it was noted that a body of Samoan parents preferred their children to learn in English, she noted:

> we have to ask ourselves how best we can "unlearn" this belief to understand the importance of language for cultural maintenance and other purposes.[48]

These views are consistent with the anti-assimilation views that arose in the 1970s in that migrants should not have to acquire the capabilities of the dominant culture. However, a closer examination of the research raises concern about the effect on education. For example, an excellent intervention targeting culturally and linguistically diverse students achieved significant improvements in outcomes.

However, when the model was replicated in schools of predominantly white students, the improvements were even greater.[49]

International studies on the effects of the language of origin on educational success are highly contestable and the evidence is still inconclusive,[50] with some papers arguing that the impact can be negative. For example, research has consistently shown that bilingual children have a smaller vocabulary in each of their languages compared to monolingual peers.[51] Similarly, bilingual adults have been found to possess more difficulties in verbal retrieval.[52]

Even the literature which supports bilingual education is often interpreted beyond what the research states. For example, Portes and Schauffler (1994) identify benefits of bilingualism, but this does not negate the importance of an English-speaking education. In fact, the research states explicitly that the 'effect of knowledge of English is very strong, exceeding four times its standard error'. Of all their measures affecting performance, 'the Knowledge of English Index has the strongest effect, dwarfing those of other predictors'.[53]

Baker (2016) studied Mexican Americans living in the United States and found that acquiring English was important for success in reading and maths achievement.[54] Baker noted that parents with strong English-language skills are more likely to pass these skills along to their children, and actually argued for programmes to teach the parents English.

Another policy that facilitates cultural diversity is the introduction of early childhood education facilities using Pacific languages and culture. These cater for children who are still at an age where their sense of culture is developing, so the normal theories about exploiting culture for cognitive scaffolding cannot apply. It is an excellent time to build language and cultural identification with the country they live in, not the one their parents left behind.

This raises the question of opportunity cost, in that if a student is weak in English, would it not be better to concentrate resources on studying English? The opportunity cost argument can draw upon Carroll's (1963) model of school learning which emphasises making best use of the limited time for learning.[55] Following this approach, a strong argument can be made for focusing on English while the proficiency lag exists.

Despite the contestable nature of the research on such programmes, cultural-based programmes are seen as a key for Pacific socio-economic advance. However, it has been noted that when bilingual classes are established in schools, it is driven by demand from parents with little regard given to the effect on education.[56] The effect on student achievement is given little consideration. This raises the need to examine barriers to cultural change in that parent's wishes to conserve their old culture are taking priority over their children's preparedness for the future. It also raises the possibility that, in promoting cultural diversity, children are not given the necessary capabilities to succeed.

Studies regularly show that Pacific students who do not have English as their main language at home have lower academic results than those who do, and Pacific languages can present obstacles to learning.[57] PISA (2006) results show that nearly half (49%) of students who did not have English as their home language were low achievers compared with only 20% from English-speaking homes.[58] This could suggest that more use should be made of Pacific languages at school so there is more commonality between home and school, but this will only disadvantage them for when they enter the English-speaking workforce.

The Department of Labour (2012) recognises the link between capabilities in the English language and income.[59] In a study of migrants to New Zealand it found that those migrants who said that English was the language they spoke best earned an income 25% higher than those who said their English was very good.

Given the importance of English-language proficiency for income, the poor performance of Pacific students is of grave concern. Compared to other ethnic groups, they are less likely to meet literacy and numeracy requirements.[60] According to one study, nearly a third of Pacific students could only complete the simplest reading tasks that PISA measures. By contrast, only 9% of European students sit in this low performance group.[61]

When searching for an explanation for these failings, the blame is placed on New Zealand teachers and the New Zealand system. In particular, the New Zealand education system is seen as failing Pacific people. New Zealand schools and teachers are identified as the cause of student failings with comments like 'many teachers and schools are not yet fully effective for Pacific students'.[62] However, there is no evidence of a more successful Pacific educational system. Pacific students may respond better to some forms of teaching, but no alternative education system exists that provides more success. In fact, outside New Zealand, the educational achievement of Pacific people is worse. In a speech to the Pacific Leader's Forum, the Minister of Foreign Affairs noted that:

- A million school-age children around the Pacific do not go to school at all.
- Around 40% of children in Pacific Island countries do not complete a basic primary education.
- Only 20% graduate from secondary school.[63]

Lobbyists and policy-makers regularly request that a Pacific style of education be provided by New Zealand teachers; however, maths and science are not traditional features of Pacific culture. There is no Pacific Island science. It was European colonialists that brought these disciplines to their shores. Hence, they could be described as a colonial infiltration yet these are important elements of a knowledge economy. Herein lies the root of the problem. Poverty is a consequence of cultural change in which some cultural groups are having to incorporate foreign cultural mechanisms, a process that can take generations.[64]

In some cases, there have been claims of institutional racism and discrimination. An example of such claims can be found in a paper entitled *Unconscious Bias in Education.* [65] This report claimed that teachers had low expectations of Maori and Pacific students and this was the cause of their under-achievement at school. The evidence for this was a survey of expectations that showed New Zealand teachers expected the best results from Asian students, followed by white Europeans,

Pasifika, then Maori. The paper argued that with such inherent bias, the schooling results were a self-fulfilling prophecy.

The problem with this paper is that Asians were at the top of the list but most New Zealand teachers are not Asian. When teachers place a different ethnic group at the top of their list, it strongly suggests that they are not biased as the report claims. If they were, we would expect white European students to be at the top. A more likely explanation for these expectations is that New Zealand teachers have learned from experience that Asians are most likely to be their best performers, while Pacific and Maori tend to perform at much lower levels. In other words, it is not the expectations of the teachers affecting performance, but the performance of the students shaping teacher expectations.

On the positive side, there are some suggestions of improvement in recent years. Gordon (2013) suggested that Pacific Islanders are among the fastest improvers in obtaining New Zealand qualification standards.[66] However, even this positive interpretation recognises that government's educational targets for Pacific students are unlikely to be met. More worryingly, these improvements occurred at a time of qualification inflation when universities criticised the declining standard of students and raised their entrance levels. Too many students who meet the official standards were failing at university. Pacific Island students were among the biggest losers when the universities changed their entrance standards.[67]

This book has stressed the importance of parental behaviours in the child's first five years, before they reach school. In line with this theme, significant differences have been noted between Pacific children and other ethnic groups in the earliest days of schooling.[68] That is to say, they are performing badly before schools and teachers have had any influence on them. This suggests we need to examine the home environment before they get to school. McNaughton (2011) claims that Pacific children have poor school readiness, which he attributes to differences in family practices and participation in early childhood education.[69]

Government ministries recognise the importance of the preschool years. The Ministry of Education identified early childhood education and family involvement as an important area of concern.[70] Similarly, the Ministry of Pacific peoples recognises the primal role of the parent–child relationship. Early childhood education is merely 'the second most important influence on children's achievement'[71] (behind parents and the family).

The problem for Pacific peoples is that they have limited experience of Western education, so lack knowledge on how best to foster it. Pacific people have migrated from islands with small market economies and low education outcomes. Furthermore, the immigration categories under which they enter New Zealand do not require high education levels. The research suggests that Pacific parents will welcome intervention. The problem is, people without experience of education lack knowledge on how to fill their behavioural gaps, as illustrated by the following quotation from a Samoan parent:

> My desire for them is to have a high level of education but I don't know what sort of support I should give my children ...[72]

Research suggests that Pacific parents will welcome improvements as they place a high value on education.[73] The problem is not values but behavioural practices. Schoeffel and Meleisea (1996) note that most Pacific Island parents want their children to do well at school, and feel disappointment about their children's educational performances. They state if a 'message directed to parents said "this is how you can help your child to achieve better at school" we believe most Polynesian parents would be interested and receptive'.[74]

One area where parental training can have an impact is in reinforcing the link between effort and achievement. Meyer et al. (2009) noted that Pacific students considered luck more important in determining their results than effort and ability.[75] Students felt they had little control over their results and had no sense of 'doing my best' associated with higher achievement. This lack of understanding of the role of effort was also observed by Jones.[76] This attitude stands in sharp contrast to the Chinese, for whom, if children have not done well, it is because they have not worked hard enough.

In the study above, the girls believed their lack of brains was the key influence over their outcomes. Such beliefs border on the biological/racial. Not only do such beliefs undermine self-esteem, they do not facilitate successful learning and achievement. This raises the potential of another danger from an under-performing ethnic group; that is, the possibility of internalising feelings of biological and/or cultural inferiority. Research normally argues that internalised racism or self-stereotyping occurs when the dominant majority's perceptions are internalised by the ethnic minority[77]; however, minority groups are capable of making their own judgements about their performance. This has important implications. When ethnic groups accept beliefs about their innate deficiencies, it can lead to low self-esteem and psychological well-being.[78]

This can further lead to adjustment mechanisms that allow students to protect their self-esteem by downplaying the importance of academic success. Schoeffel and Meleisea (1996) found examples of peer pressure among students not to show too much liking for their teachers, and of the need to affect a 'don't-care' attitude.[79] This finding shows similarities to Ogbu's (1978) notion of oppositional identity and Lewis's (1966) culture of poverty in the United States.[80]

Herein lies a danger of not dealing with this issue. If an ethnic group becomes marginalised for a long enough period of time, they may adopt behavioural practices and values that propagate failure, and society becomes stratified with class based on ethnicity.

Notes

1 Rickman, J. (attributed) (1785). *Journal of Captain Cook's Last Voyage to the Pacific Ocean on the Discovery: Performed in the Years 1776, 1777, 1778, 1779 and 1780.* London: E Newbery, p. 53.
2 Bedggood, D. (1978). New Zealand's semi-colonial development: A Marxist view. *The Australian and New Zealand Journal of Sociology, 14*(3), 285–289.
3 Cited in Salmond (1997), p. 415.

4 Best, E. (1934). *The Maori as He Was: A Brief Account of Maori Life as it Was in Pre-European Days*. Wellington: New Zealand Board of Science and Art, pp. 4–6.
5 Ibid., p. 8.
6 Jenkins, K., & Harte, H.M. (2011). *Traditional Maori Parenting: An Historical Review of Literature of Traditional Maori Child Rearing Practices in Pre-European Times*. Auckland: Te Kahui Mana Ririki.
7 Ibid, p. 24.
8 Forster, J. cited in Hoare, M. (Ed.) (1982). *The Resolution Journal of Johann Reinhold Forster* (1729–98) III. Melbourne: Hawthorn Press, p. 419.
9 Forster, G. (1777). *A Voyage around the World in His Britannic Majesties Sloop Resolution*. London: B. White. I, pp. 496–497.
10 Barry, Child & Bacon (1959).
11 Firth, R. (1972). *Economics of the New Zealand Maori*. Wellington, NZ: A. R. Shearer, Government Printer, p. 189.
12 Cited in Ward, A.D. (1958). The History of the East Coast Maori Trust. Unpublished Ph.D. thesis, Victoria University, p. 149.
13 Lady Martin (1884) *Our Maoris*. London: Society for Promoting Christian Knowledge, p. 10.
14 Ibid., pp. 109, 31 and 72.
15 Stout-Ngata Commission. (1907). G-1c, Wellington: Appendices to the Journals of the House of Representatives, p. 14.
16 Native Land Laws Commission Evidence AJHR. (1891). G-1, xxx. Wellington, NZ, Appendices to the Journals of the House of Representatives, p.168.
17 Ibid.
18 Stout-Ngata Commission (1907), p. 21.
19 Firth (1972), p.467.
20 Love. N. (1998–99). Maori development: Issues and solutions. *International Policy Review*, *8*, 42–60, p. 51.
21 Sorenson, M. P. K. (1981). Maori and Pakeha. In W. H. Oliver & B. R. Williams (Eds.), *The Oxford History of New Zealand*. Wellington, NZ: Oxford University Press, pp. 168–193.
22 Department of Corrections. (2017). *Annual Report 2016–7*. Wellington: Department of Corrections.
23 The Modernising Child Youth and Family Expert Panel. (2015). *Expert Panel Final Report: Investing in New Zealand's Children and Their Families*. Wellington: Ministry of Social Development.
24 Department of Corrections (2017).
25 Department of Corrections (2017), p. 57.
26 Macpherson, C. (1977). Polynesians in New Zealand: An emerging eth-class? In D. Pitt (Ed.), *Social Class in New Zealand*. Auckland: Longman Paul, pp. 99–112, p.107.
27 MacPherson (1977), p. 99.
28 Bedford, R., Macpherson, C., & Spoonley, P. (2000). *Divided City? Tangata Pasifika in a New Zealand Metropolis*. Population Studies Centre Discussion paper, No. 36, October, p. 19.
29 Perry, B. (2013). *Household Incomes in New Zealand: Trends in Indicators of Inequality and Hardship 1982 to 2012*. Wellington: Ministry of Social Development, p. 131.
30 Statistics NZ. (2013). *2013 Census Quick Stats about National Highlights*. Wellington: Statistics NZ.
31 McNaughton and Lai (2008), p. 55.
32 Laban, L. (2007a). *Overcoming the Barriers Facing Our Small Pacific Communities*, 12 April. Downloaded from http://www.beehive.govt.nz/node/29001.
33 Laban L. (2007b). *Pacific People's Connectedness*. 2 April. Downloaded from http://www.beehive.govt.nz/node/28885.

34 Fletcher, M., & Dwyer. M. (2008). *A Fair Go for All Children: Actions to Address Poverty in New Zealand*. A report for the Children's Commissioner and Barnardo's.
35 Collins (2012).
36 Perry (2013).
37 Child Poverty Monitor (2013).
38 State Services Commission, The Treasury and the Department of the Prime Minister and Cabinet. (2011). *Performance Improvement Framework: Formal Review: Ministry of Pacific Island Affairs*. Wellington: The Author.
39 Ministry of Education (n.d). *Pasifika Education Plan*. Wellington: Ministry of Education. Downloaded from http://www.minedu.govt.nz/NZEducation/EducationPolicies/PasifikaEducation/~/media/MinEdu/Files/EducationSectors/PasifikaEducation/PasifikaEdPlan2013To2017V2.pdf.
40 Schoeffel, P., & Meleisea, M. (1996). Pacific Islands Polynesian attitudes to child training and discipline in New Zealand: Some policy implications for social welfare and education. *Social Policy Journal of New Zealand, 6*, 134–147.
41 Mila-Schaaf, K., & Robinson, E. (2010). Polycultural capital and educational achievement among NZ-born Pacific peoples. *Mai Review, 1*, 1–18.
42 Portes, A., & Schauffler, R. (1994). Language and the second generation: Bilingualism yesterday and today. *International Migration Review, 28*, 640–661.
43 Garcia, G.E. (2000). Bilingual students' reading. In M. Kamil, P. Mosenthal, P.D. Pearson, & R. Barr (Eds.), *Handbook of Reading Research*, vol. 3. Mahwah, NJ: Erlbaum, pp. 813–834; Sweet, A.P., & Snow, C.E. (2003). *Rethinking Reading Comprehension*. New York: Guilford Press.
44 Fletcher et al. (2006).
45 Amituanai-Toloa, M., McNaughton, S., & Lai, M.K. (2008). Reading comprehension in English for Samoan bilingual students in Samoan classes. *New Zealand Journal of Educational Studies, 43*, 5–20.
46 Amituanai-Toloa, M., McNaughton, S., Lai, M.K., & Airini. (2009). Milestone 4, Pasifika Schooling Improvement Project. Unpublished draft report to the Ministry of Education, Wellington.
47 Amituanai-Toloa, M. (2010). To each a language: Addressing the challenges of language and cultural loss for Samoans. *AlterNative: An International Journal of Indigenous Peoples, 6*, 79.
48 Amituanai-Toloa (2010), p. 83.
49 McNaughton, S., & Lai, M.K. (2008). A model of school change for culturally and linguistically diverse students in New Zealand: A summary and evidence from systematic replication. *Teaching Education, 20*, 55–75.
50 Kristen et al. (2011).
51 Oller, D.K., & Eilers, R.E. (Eds.). (2002). *Language and Literacy in Bilingual Children*. Clevedon: Multilingual Matters.
52 Kaushanskaya, M., & Marian, V. (2007). Bilingual language processing and interference in bilinguals: Evidence from eye tracking and picture naming. *Language Learning, 57*, 119–163.
53 Portes & Schauffler (1994), p. 658.
54 Baker (2016).
55 Carroll, J.B. (1963). A model of school learning. *Teachers College Record, 64*, 723–733.
56 Amituanai-Toloa (2010).
57 Franken, M., May, S., & McComish, J. (2005). *Leap (Language Enhancing the Achievement of Pasifika): Literature Review*. Downloaded from http://education.waikato.ac.nz/research/report/index.php?id=64.
58 PISA. (2006). *Program for International Student Assessment 2006*. Paris: OECD.
59 Department of Labour. (2012). *Labour Market Integration of Recent Migrants in New Zealand*. Wellington: Department of Labour.

60 Statistics NZ and Ministry of Pacific Island Affairs. (2010). *Education and Pacific Peoples in New Zealand.* Wellington: Authors.
61 Cited in Statistics NZ et al. (2010).
62 Ibid., p. 37.
63 McCully, M. (2011). Speech on Pacific Development, 5 September 2011. Downloaded from http://www.voxy.co.nz/politics/speech-murray-mccully-pacific-development/5/100388.
64 Clydesdale, G. (2017). *The Politically Correct Economy.* Christchurch: Craft Publications.
65 Houkamau, C., Blank, A., & Kingi, H. (2016). *Unconscious Bias and Education.* Downloaded from https://www.ncsehe.edu.au/wp-content/uploads/2016/11/Carla-Houkamau-Unconscious-Bias-and-Education-Slides.pdf.
66 Gordon, L. (2013). *Who Achieves What in Secondary Schooling? A Conceptual and Empirical Analysis.* New Zealand Post Primary Teachers' Association (PPTA).
67 Downes, S. (2015). University entrance rates down, NCEA pass rates up. *Dominion Post*, 8 July.
68 McNaughton, S., Phillips, G., & MacDonald, S. (2000). Curriculum channels and literacy development over the first year of instruction. *New Zealand Journal of Educational Studies, 35*, 49–59.
69 Ibid.
70 Ministry of Education (n.d.)
71 Statistics NZ et al. (2010), p. 14.
72 Amituanai-Toloa et al. (2009), p. 17.
73 Wylie, C., Hodgen, E., & Darr, C. (2009). *National Standards Consultation Analysis.* Report for the Ministry of Education. Wellington: Ministry of Education.
74 Schoeffel & Meleisea (1996), p. 145.
75 Meyer, L.H., Weir, K.F., McClure, J., Walkey, F., & McKenzie, L. (2009). *Motivation and Achievement at Secondary School: The Relationship between NCEA Design and Student Motivation and Achievement: A Three-year Follow-up.* Report for the Ministry of Education by the Jessie Heterington Centre for Educational Research and the School of Psychology – Victoria University of Wellington, July 2009. Wellington: Ministry of Education.
76 Jones cited in Franken et al. (2005).
77 For example, Williams, D.R., & Mohammed, S.A. (2013). Racism and health I: Pathways and scientific evidence. *American Behavioral Scientist, 57*(8), 1152–1173.
78 Kwate, N.O.A., & Meyer, I.H. (2011). On sticks and stones and broken bones: Stereotypes and African American health. *Du Bois Review: Social Science Research on Race, 8*, 191–198.
79 Schoeffel & Meleisea (1996).
80 Ogbu (1978); Lewis (1966).

11 Poverty vs welfare

This book is based upon the idea that a lack of material resources reduces life quality, but is that true? There is a significant body of research on this topic but this chapter will limit itself to a few pertinent points.

The United Nations certainly sees a link between poverty and welfare. In the foreward to the Human Development Report 2000, the UN's development programme administrator Mark Malloch Brown stated:

> to be poor is to be powerless and vulnerable. Life remains a torment for children in the teeming barrio of a developing country city, for refugees caught up on a conflict, for women in a society that still denies them equality and freedom every day brings physical and psychological threats. And still too many of the 1.2 billion people living on less than a dollar a day lack even the most basic human security.[1]

But is this statement correct? Could it be an example of Western people valuing materialism and assuming those without material assets are impoverished? The idea that resources make a significant difference in welfare is a key assumption in the battle against poverty, or to put it another way, money makes you happy. However, many people would dispute this. For example, Tännsjö (1998) states:

> The view that I am prepared to defend is somewhat pessimistic but still, I am afraid, realistic. My impression is that if only our basic needs are satisfied, then most of us are capable of living lives that, on balance, are worth experiencing. However, no matter how "lucky" we are, how many "gadgets" we happen to possess, we rarely reach beyond this level ...[2]

Of course, Tännsjö is not writing off materialism completely. He argues that we need enough resources to meet our basic needs; the problem is that even the definition of basic needs varies between cultures.

A number of writers have found a strong link between income and happiness.[3] On average, those on higher incomes are, at any given time, happier than those on lower incomes.[4] Those on higher incomes have resources to overcome the problems that confront them in life. Poorer people do not have this buffer and this affects their psychological state.[5]

But maybe this reflects control, not wealth. One line of research argues that people who are dependent on others for resources have less control over their own lives. Psychologists have found a strong link between happiness, welfare and a feeling of control. The events that have the biggest negative impact on our welfare are those that threaten our sense of control.[6] Such events create a sense of powerlessness, helplessness and a feeling of being at the mercy of the environment.

One pioneering study of happiness in Africa was conducted by Biswas-Deiner, Vitterso and Diener in 2005.[7] They attempted to measure 'subjective well-being' of the Maasai in Kenya. Subjective Well-being refers to how individuals evaluate the quality of their own lives. To do this, the researchers surveyed ten villages in South-Western Kenya. The people in these communities had resisted colonial incursions into their culture. They lived a traditional pastoralist life and had retained most of their pre-colonial language, values and practices.

The list of traditional practices may shock many Westerners. It included polygamy, child marriages, circumcision of young adults, and a period of warrior-hood for young men. The economy was very basic and, by Western standards, these people were very poor. Their simple houses were made from mud, sticks and dung. This was not a knowledge economy and did not produce the wealth that such an economy produces. Western-style learning was not a feature of life and the children did not receive the 'benefits' of attending school nor modern media. They did not even engage in a cash-market economy. It was a herding style bereft of all modern advantages.

This description suggests that these people needed to escape their impoverished existence and academics should intervene to help them. However, the researchers did not find the despair we might expect. In fact, they found the opposite, the Maasai were very happy. The researchers measured happiness in a number of ways including cognitive and emotional evaluations and their research consistently found that without Western intervention and resource levels, the Maasai were still happy.

An interesting feature of these findings is that the Maasai appear to rank low on other aspects of welfare that have little to do with poverty. The biologist Robert Sapolsky studied wildlife in Africa and lived among cultures that share features with the Maasai. In his book *Behave* he describes people he encountered ...

> who believe that epileptics are possessed and that the organs of murdered albinos have healing powers, where beating of wives, children and animals is the norm, five year olds herd cattle and haul fire wood, pubescent girls are clitoridectomized and given to old men as third wives.[8]

Sapolsky also notes the importance of the Enlightenment in delivering societal changes that enhanced welfare. He notes that:

> countries with minimal violence, extensive social safety nets, few child brides, numerous female legislators and sacrosanct civil liberties are usually direct descendants of the enlightenment.[9]

This raises a number of serious questions. Firstly, are the people who want to reduce poverty, including myself, trapped within our own cultural schema? Secondly, is there a possibility that if Africans were left alone, they might be happy or even happier? Could interventions, including the ones suggested in this book actually reduce welfare and happiness?

A famous guide to welfare policy was provided by John Rawls who suggested that when we assess the distribution of wealth in society, we do so behind a veil of ignorance in which we don't know our position in that society.[10] This ignorance tends to lift our generosity as we imagine how hard life would be if we were at the bottom. However, we make those judgements within our own cultural schemas which may not be so relevant when assessing other cultures.

The finding that Maasai were happy despite being poor is not unique. For example, Biswas-Diener and Diener studied slums in Calcutta;[11] in other words, the poorest of the poor. If the UN report cited at the beginning of this chapter is correct, we would expect people in this situation to be living a miserable life and the researchers did find a slightly negative welfare for the most marginalised groups. However, in some areas of their lives, they found positive satisfaction. Overall, the marginalised poor were around neutral in life satisfaction. They were not miserable.

Cox (2012) studied the marginalised poor in Nicaragua and found similar results.[12] The urban and rural poor, including dump dwellers, were about neutral on life satisfaction. The only people reporting dramatically low life-satisfaction were the sex workers who also had to endure negative social stigma. This is a reminder that resources are not the only source of welfare and others exist. One of the most important for the Nicaraguan poor were their strong social relations.

These findings suggest that poverty does not equal misery and the statement above by the United Nations Development Programme administrator dramatically over-state the negative effect of low resources. Poverty does not equal misery. The marginalised poor are not living dramatically unhappy, unsatisfying or unfulfilled lives.[13]

This raises the question 'why aren't poor people miserable?' Academics have offered a number of explanations and one of them is simply that people adapt to their situation. For example, De Frain and Ernst (1978) studied parents who had gone through the pain of losing a child.[14] They found that, when the child died, the parents experienced a significant drop in happiness; however, over time they adapted and after two to three years their happiness levels recovered to what it had been.

Another explanation argues that much of our happiness is biologically driven and not affected by changes in our external circumstances. This view has been supported by a number of studies including a study of twins by Lykken and Tellegen[14]. Twins share similar genetic structure and the researchers found they also share strong similarities in their reported well-being. In fact, the well-being of an identical twin was found to be a better indicator of happiness than education, income or status. Hence the researchers suggested that so strong are we biologically determined that 'trying to be happier is as futile as trying to be taller and therefore is counterproductive'.[15] This suggests that little of our situation determines happiness, including our resource level.

This led to the idea of a happiness 'set-point' which suggests that although we can experience some variation, our happiness over time is relatively stable. People's happiness levels do not vary much. As Liszka states 'making decisions on the basis of supposed increments or decrements of happiness is bad policy criteria and bad ethics'.[16] We may get a burst of happiness when we buy that new car, but we soon return to normal and gain little happiness over the Maasai in Kenya. Not only does this imply the pursuit of money is a false dream but that policies aimed at giving people more money will not significantly enhance happiness.

However, more recent research does not support the set-point theory. An individual's happiness can vary substantially throughout their life and environmental circumstances can have a major impact on this. When people experience adversity, their happiness drops[17] and although they may adapt over time, they do not always return to their previous level of happiness. Some happiness may be biological or internal, but we are not completely immune to situational factors.[18]

We are particularly vulnerable to negative experiences over which we have no control. Hence, Veenhoven suggests that, when considering well-being, we should focus on negative living conditions that are beyond an individual's control. We can see under this logic, rationale for policies that provide a 'safety net' and also humanitarian/disaster aid. But does it justify policies that make people richer?[19]

A large body of research has reported a strong relationship between happiness and wealth, especially for the poor.[20] It seems that for those with low incomes and few assets, money can make a difference. However, the benefit of extra money declines as people gets richer. It appears that people need enough resources to meet their basic needs, but beyond that, the gains to happiness become smaller and smaller.[21]

This would suggest that happiness and welfare of a country's population could be increased if the rich were taxed and the money redistributed to the poor. However, it isn't quite that simple and depends on a number of factors. For example, if the rich made their money from hard work the taxation could reduce their happiness. And if the poor believe in a meritocracy, they too may become less happy with the changes in the social-economic system. More importantly, if the tax system acts as a disincentive to production, all members of society can be come poorer and there will be less money to share around.

Another problem is the relationship between wealth and happiness is not linear nor universal. In fact, in Argentina those in the lower echelons of society report greater happiness than those in the upper classes.[22] Another contradiction can be found in Bangladesh which is one of the poorest countries in the world. However, its inhabitants are often reported happier than those living in more affluent countries.[23] It seems that cultural, social and other factors can have a significant impact on our happiness.[24]

Research may vary in their findings because of how happiness is measured. For example, if people are asked to cognitively evaluate their life satisfaction, there may be greater emphasis on income and wealth. However, if they are to report on their emotions or feelings, psycho-social needs come to the fore.[25] That is to say the quality of our relationships can keep us happy regardless of our material situation, and similarly those with material wealth may be unhappy because of the state of their relationships.

Cognitive assessments can also vary in the way that satisfaction is evaluated. In Western nations, it is common for people to assess their current well-being by comparing it to what they had in the past.[26] So, if their situation has improved over time, they are more likely to be happy. This phenomenon could be found in China. A study of Chinese farmers found they regularly compared their current situation to what they had in the past.[27] This suggests that poor people can be happy as long as they have improved their position over time.

Another way that people evaluate their well-being is by comparing their lives to others. This practice of social comparison is found throughout the world and suggests poorer people will feel worse if they have less than those around them. But is jealousy a sufficient reason for growing incomes?

Of course, poverty is more than jealousy. Amartya Sen states that life quality is enhanced when people have the capabilities and freedoms that enable them to lead flourishing lives.[28] We can assume that people with resources are in a better position to live a fulfilled life; however, there are cultural variations in what people consider fulfilling. For example, many cultures get great fulfilment from hunting and gathering foods, yet the Westerners who make the measures of happiness do not value these capabilities and freedoms. In fact, they may see these actions in negative terms given their effect on bio-diversity.

This can also be seen in the United Nation's measure of development. The Human Development Index (HDI) measures real income, lifespan and education and it provides a close correlation with subjective well-being in European nations.[29] However, the education in this index is a Western-style education, not that provided by village elders. Its measure of real income favours market-based economies so that cultures with cultivated land and traded output are preferred to natural environments where hunting occurs, as the later does not contribute to GDP.

Herein lies a problem with this book. There is no doubt that the Western socio-economic system has generated greater wealth, and those with wealth tend to be happier than those who are poor. However, too much cultural shift may reduce life quality, especially when dealing with something as personal as the family. In fact, the biggest barrier to 'improvement' may not come from discriminatory or biased institutions, but from those inside their culture who don't want to change. Should we judge these people with Western perceptions of poverty and what constitutes wealth?

Notes

1 Human Development Report (2000). *Human Development Report 2000*, New Delhi: Oxford University Press.

2 Tännsjö, T. (1998). *Hedonistic Utilitarianism*. Edinburgh: Edinburgh University Press, p. 161.

3 Argyle, M. (1999). Causes and correlates of happiness. In D. Kahneman, E. Diener, & N. Schwarz (Eds.), *Well-Being: The Foundations of Hedonic Psychology*. New York: Russell Sage Foundation, pp. 353–373.
4 Easterlin, R. (2001) Income and happiness: Towards a unified theory. *The Economic Journal, 111*(473), 465–484.
5 West, C.G., Reed, D.M., & Gildengorin, G.L. (1998). Can money buy happiness? Depressive symptoms in an affluent older population. *Journal of The American Geriatrics Society, 46*(1), 49–57.
6 Mcfarlane, A.H., Norman, G.R., Streiner, D.L., & Roy, R.G. (1983). The process of social stress: Stable, reciprocal and mediating relationships. *Journal of Health and Social Behaviour, 24*, 160–173.
7 Biswas-Deiner, R., Vitterso, J., & Diener, E. (2005). Most people are pretty happy but there is cultural variation: The Inughuit, the Amish and the Maasai. *Journal of Happiness Studies, 6*, 205–226.
8 Sapolsky, R.M. (2017). *Behave: The Biology of Humans at Our Best and Worst*. New York: Penguin, p. 616.
9 Ibid., p. 617.
10 Rawls, J. (1973). *A Theory of Justice*. Oxford: Oxford University Press.
11 Biswas-Diener, R., & Diener, E. (2001). Making the best of a bad situation: Satisfaction in the slums of Calcutta. *Social Indicators Research, 55*, 329–352.
12 Cox, K. (2012). Happiness and unhappiness in the developing world: Life satisfaction among sex workers, dump-dwellers, urban poor, and rural peasants in Nicaragua. *Journal of Happiness Studies, 13*(1), 103–128.
13 Ibid.; Clydesdale, G. (2015). Happiness, welfare and ethics: Dissonant consequences and conflicting values. *International Journal of Happiness and Development, 2*(2), 137–159.
14 De Frain, J., & Ernst, L. (1978). The psychological effects of sudden infant death syndrome on surviving family members. *Journal of Family Practice, 6*(5), 985–989.
15 Lykken, D., & Tellegen, A. (1996). Happiness is a stochastic phenomenon. *Psychological Science, 7*, 186–189.
16 Ibid.
17 Liszka, J. (2005). Why happiness is of marginal value in ethical decision making. *Journal of Value Inquiry, 39*, 325–344, p. 341.
18 Mirowsky, J., & Ross, C.E. (2003). *Social Causes of Psychological Distress*. New York: Walter de Gruyter.
19 Veenhoven, R. (1994). Is happiness a trait? Tests of the theory that a better society does not make people any happier. *Social Indicators Research, 32*, 101–160.
20 Howell, R.T., & Howell, C.J. (2008). The relation of economic status to subjective well-being in developing countries: A meta-analysis. *Psychological Bulletin, 134*, 536–560; Diener, E., & Biswas-Diener, R. (2002). Will money increase subjective well-being? A literature review and guide to needed research. *Social Indicators Research, 57*, 119–169.
21 Veenhoven, R. (1993). *Happiness in Nations: Subjective Appreciation of Life in 56 Nations*. Rotterdam: Risbo.
22 Haller, M., & Hadler, M. (2006). How social relations and structures can produce happiness and unhappiness: An interpersonal comparative analysis. *Social Indicators Research, 75*, 169–216.
23 Camfield, L., Choudhury, K., & Devine, J. (2009). Well-being, happiness, and why relationships matter: Evidence from Bangladesh. *Journal of Happiness Studies, 10*, 71–91.
24 Cox (2012).
25 Tay, L., & Deiner, E. (2011). Needs and subjective well-being around the world. *Journal of Personality and Social Psychology, 101*(2), 354–365; Diener, E., Ng, W., Harter, J., & Arora, R. (2010). Wealth and happiness across the world: Material

prosperity predicts life evaluation, whereas psychosocial prosperity predicts positive feeling. *Journal of Personality and Social Psychology, 99*(1), 52–61.
26 Michalos, A.C. (1985). Multiple discrepancies theory (MDT). *Social Indicators Research, 16*, 347–413.
27 Davey, G., Chen, Z., & Lau, A. (2009). Peace in a thatched hut – that is happiness: Subjective wellbeing among peasants in rural China. *Journal of Happiness Studies, 10*, 239–252.
28 Sen, A. (1991). *Development and Freedom.* Oxford: Oxford University Press.
29 Blanchflower, D.G., & Oswald, A.J. (2011). *International Happiness.* NBER Working Paper No. w16668. Downloaded from SSRN: http://ssrn.com/abstract=1737216.

12 Do we really want to solve this?

The incomes earned by any individual are strongly influenced by their educational outcomes, and the main influence on this is their home environment and parental practice. This book argues that parental practice is influenced by culture and the inheritance of behaviours from previous generations. This view is consistent with evolutionary economics which focuses on routines/behaviours. It recognises that cultural change involves acquisition of new routines, and in some cases the downplaying of old routines. It is not suggested that this is the only explanation and solution for poverty, but given our poor results to date, there is a need to expand our repertoire of solutions.

To avoid poverty, human capital is needed that enables an individual to build wealth and income. This places an emphasis on education, the primary influences of which are parental/family and quality of schooling. Education prepares youth for the socio-economic system in which they will spend the rest of their lives, but some behaviours that ethnic groups bring with them are more suited to the system they or their ancestors lived in.

In some cases, an ethnic minority may possess behavioural repertoires that allow greater success, as seen in the case of Asian educational outcomes. The contrast between Chinese and Pacific was notable. Some Pacific students have stated that they lack brains and do not grasp the link between effort and achievement. By contrast, for Chinese, brains are irrelevant. There is huge emphasis on effort and if a student does not perform well, s/he has not worked hard enough.

The Chinese parents referred to in this book have higher educational achievements and were aware of what behaviours contribute to educational success. They possess a behavioural repertoire that Pacific parents lack, but acquiring behaviours is difficult unless they are exposed to them. Herein lies a policy solution. The government needs programmes that help parents acquire those behaviours.

In 2011, Nobel Prize winner James Heckman examined inequality in America and called for policy to shift and focus on the core skills needed for success in life.[1] He noted that these skills are formed before children enter school and are a consequence of parental practice. Heckman did not say discrimination does not have an influence on economic outcomes, but noted that it is of secondary importance to the skills that minority groups bring to the labour market. He states that 'any serious accounting of economic and social disparities must reckon with the importance of skills in American society'.[2]

Heckman, Stixrud and Urzua (2006) noted that there are differences in cognitive and non-cognitive abilities between racial groups in the United States that begin early and persist through life, thereby contributing to socio-economic outcomes.[3] Schools do little to reduce this gap. These gaps appear when children enter school. These observations of American children are similar to those made by McNaughton and his colleagues (2000, 2011) of Maori and Pacific Island children in New Zealand.[4]

Heckman called for American policy to shift and focus on the core skills needed for success in life which are formed before children enter school, by focusing on parenting. He states 'Parenting matters. The true measure of child poverty and advantage is the quality of parenting a child receives, not just the money available to a household.'[5]

However, policies of targeting parents have received significant resistance. Heckman (2011) noted how a report by Moynahan (1965) which focused on the African American families was criticised for 'blaming the victim'.[6] Similarly, Coleman et al. (1966) published a report that showed it was families, not schools, that were the principal determinant of schooling outcomes.[7] However, Heckman laments that 'After 40 years, the wisdom of Coleman and Moynihan has not yet been incorporated into American public policy. Yet, their message is clear. Family matters.'[8]

A reluctance to focus policy on the family has also been observed in New Zealand. A paper prepared for the Ministry of Pacific Island Affairs noted:

> rather than adopting a deficit conception of Pasifika peoples, their communities, cultures and/or languages – as has been characteristic of much public policy towards Pasifika peoples in the past – we need to examine the adequacy of the institutional provision of key services, such as education, and the degree to which such institutional provision supports the aspirations and trajectories of Pasifika peoples in New Zealand.[9]

An interesting observation of the previous case study was the statement from the academic who, on observing that Samoan parents were wanting their children to learn in English, wanted the parents to 'unlearn' this idea. Yet, the children will live in an English-speaking economy where English ability will impact on the income they earn.

Another interesting observation was that parents stressing the need for traditional language instruction did not give any consideration to the effect this would have on the child's education and achievement. This reproduction of past behaviour is consistent with academic literature that shows persistence often occurs without full assessment of the efficiency of those behaviours.[10] This drive to maintain the culture of the parents is supported by government institutions which place a premium on maintaining cultural diversity.

Cultures can be very resistant to change. Economists have documented a number of forms of inertia that restrict change. A society's skills, capabilities and knowledge has been built up over time and cannot be changed easily; a problem compounded by Polanyi's (1967) observation that much knowledge is tacit and cannot be easily acquired.[11] Some tacit knowledge can only be acquired by experience and cannot be easily be transferred. It can also be hard to transfer technologies between countries. Because production technologies are the result of a nation's peculiar ideologies, cultures, historical experience and language, they are country specific and are not easily transferable.[12]

Barriers to change also include motivational effects. Levinson (1978) describes the pain of loss, the uncertainty and fear of failure as barriers to changing existing life structures.[13] Lost opportunities, losing power struggles, and failure all serve to dampen motivation for change. Levinson also suggests fear of losing control of the situation under the new regime. This may explain why Pacific parents wanted their children to learn in their home language and did not consider the effect on the child's education.

Stakeholders can be particularly powerful barriers to change. People with expertise based on the old ways will no longer be perceived as experts.[14] They may use their remaining expert status to resist change and therefore protect their status and power base. This may also be driven by income. Olson (1982) states that, over time, a stable society will build up a number of distributional coalitions – entities that are 'overwhelmingly oriented to struggles over the distribution of income and wealth than to the production of additional output'.[15] A change may undermine their income.

Another possible explanation for resistance may be a poor understanding of material prosperity. Consequently, policy-makers have concentrated on structural and distributional solutions. The natural state of human-kind is not one of prosperity. It is one of poverty. The knowledge-based innovations that grew out of Western Europe are unique in human history. It is the exception to the rule, and by comparison, all other humans have lived in relative poverty, as their ancestors had, and their ancestors before them.

Knowledge and capabilities are needed to build prosperity and remove material poverty. Hence, this book argues that our view of human capital must be extended. We must also consider the capabilities to acquire capabilities, and the importance of parental behaviours in this process.

Another barrier to change comes for academics. For decades sociologists refused to consider the possibility that culture could be a determinant of poverty. Vaisey (2010) states that most social scientists do not accept that culture plays a significant role in perpetuating socio-economic disadvantage; the primary reason being an aversion to 'blaming the victim'.[16] Consequently, research has focused on social-structural factors with little attention given to cultural determinants of failure. Similarly, Kao and Thompson (2003) claim that cultural models are popular for explaining the high performance of Asians, but they are out of favour when explaining lower performance groups.[17] This selective use of culture means that social scientists may be missing their best opportunity to solve poverty in marginalised ethnic groups.

A notable exemption was Oscar Lewis who, in 1966, published a report that a culture of poverty among Puerto Ricans.[18] However, he was chastised by other academics for doing so. As Princeton Professor Douglas Massey notes:

> in my view, sociology did itself a grave disservice when it demonized and ostracized Lewis following the 1966 publication of his book, *La Vida: A Puerto Rican Family in the Culture of Poverty*, for which he was vilified and accused of 'blaming the victim'. For decades, it was not possible to use culture and poverty in the same sentence in polite sociological company.[19]

With this in mind, it is important to differentiate between blame and causation. No one can be blamed if their homeland was cut off from global knowledge flows by the Sahara Desert or Pacific Ocean. Nor can they be blamed if they were born into a non-literate society, and no one can be blamed if the parental methods they practice are the same they learned from their parents and others around them. Causation does not mean blame.

Culture is not economically neutral, and cultures vary significantly in their ability to create material wealth. Material poverty is the absence of material wealth, and if we genuinely want to solve material poverty, we need to recognise where some cultures may be deficient.

Each culture creates its own mechanisms for exploiting the resource base on which that culture relies. If you take someone endowed with some cultural behaviours, routines and capabilities, then place them in a different culture and resource base, they may not have the skills to succeed. It might be expected that immigrants adapt the required behaviours in their new society. However cultural mechanisms are passed on through the parents and some are not easily changed, especially if migration occurs in large enough numbers, and the old cultural behaviours are reinforced in regional sub-cultures.

A need for greater variety in policy tools

> An economically advantaged child exposed to low-quality parenting is more disadvantaged than an economically disadvantaged child exposed to high-quality parenting.[20]
>
> (Nobel Prize winner James Heckman)

Material poverty reflects an absence of material wealth and, in the eighteenth century, a revolution occurred in Europe that made all other cultures look poor by comparison. Europeans began to use knowledge systematically to improve productivity and the welfare of its citizens. This led to the creation of a knowledge economy which required higher cognitive skills than resource-based economies.

Economies that took the lead in wealth creation also stressed self-discipline, high literacy skills and time management. These features have a corollary with what developmental psychologists stress, that is the need for strong language and vocabulary, structure, social skills and self-control.

Developmental and educational psychologists have long recognised the prime role that parenting and the family environment has on children's academic outcomes. That academic achievement then influences the qualifications and incomes they will earn in later life. The first five years of their life lays the foundation for their later outcomes.[21] Consequently, there is a direct link between parenting and poverty. In economic terms, parenting lays the foundation of human capital development.

This book advocates parental programmes as a remedy. However, this policy line has several limitations and care must be taken in how these courses are conducted. Some parents who have experienced a lifetime of marginalisation may have developed self-defeating beliefs including lack of confidence and belief that they can improve. The extent that these barriers exist will vary from individual to individual. Some may have these barriers; some may not, and those that do may vary in their intensity. Nevertheless, if they do exist, they need to be recognised and overcome. At the same time, care is needed to not to appear patronising and falsely raise self-esteem.

Second, there are many ways to bring up a child successfully.[22] However, academia has a tendency to form orthodoxies. Those of us with a concern for poverty need to be flexible in policy application with openness to diverse views.

Each ethnic group may require its own policy application. The history of any ethnic group is different to others, hence they will have different causes of poverty and will require different solutions. For example, African Americans have suffered from significant discrimination and until recent decades, the possibility of obtaining top paying jobs was unobtainable. In which case, discrimination has had an important influence. By contrast, Polynesian migrants to New Zealand have genuinely experienced better economic outcomes in New Zealand than in their home countries, but nevertheless experience poorer economic outcomes compared to most New Zealanders.

Because of historical variation, the descriptions and solutions may not apply to all ethnic groups to the same degree. When examining African Americans, there is no doubt that discrimination has had a significant impact. But this discrimination may have had yet another deep impact, and a subject for future research would be the extent to which being denied jobs that require higher education affected parental practices and goals. If it did have an effect, previous racial practices did not just affect African Americans at the time discrimination was strongest, it may have impeded the adoption of practices that would affect future generations

It must also be noted that parental practice has changed over the last two hundred years. Perhaps the best evidence of this is the large number of books on parental practice. In this light, ethnic groups have not just had to catch up. They must catch up with people who are themselves improving their parental skills.

A limitation of the argument in this book is the need to recognise variation in economies. There is good reason why parenting skills evolved to suit the economy/resource base in which people live. To impose a Western parenting model, designed for a knowledge economy, on a traditional agricultural economy could be counter-productive. Some practices might benefit from being transferred but there is also a danger of a mis-match of skills. This reiterates an issue identified earlier, that is, it is not a case of superior or inferior parenting. It is a case of being fit for purpose.

This issue is particularly complex for emerging economies. These economies are not yet fully developed 'knowledge economies'. They are in the process of transition so replacing existing parental/educational practices with those required in Europe or the United States may not be beneficial. It may result in over-education and unemployment. This puts policy-makers in a quandary. Education and parental practices must meet the needs of the existing economy, but it must also provide the human capital for transition.

Even in Western societies, there are reports of over-education. Improvements in human capital have not been matched by an increase in economic growth. With this in mind, it is important to note that this book is not about economic growth per se. It provides an explanation of why some ethnic groups are in intergenerational poverty and what must be done to reduce that situation.

There is still much work to be done in this area, including recognition of the limits of these remedies. For example, if children are provided too much structure, do they lose the ability to be flexible in situations without structure? Similarly, how many educational resources are necessary? Is there are point at which no extra gain is made from additional resources?

Finally, it is also important to note that this book does not advocate full-scale or enforced assimilation. The emphasis is on the optional acquisition of new behaviours, and only those behaviours linked to poverty are targeted. This leaves ethnic groups free to practise their diverse activities and beliefs. In fact, if governments assist the acquisition of wealth generating behaviours, ethnic minorities may end up more prosperous and therefore in a better position to preserve other important aspects of their culture.

Notes

1 Heckman, J.J. (2011). The American family in Black and White: A post-racial strategy for improving skills to promote equality. *Daedalus, 140*, 70–89.
2 Ibid., p. 12.
3 Heckman, J.J., Stixrud, J., & Urzua, S. (2006). *The Effects of Cognitive and Non-cognitive Abilities on Labor Market Outcomes and Social Behavior* (No. w12006). National Bureau of Economic Research.
4 McNaughton et al. (2000); McNaughton, S. (2011). Educational outcomes in adolescence for Māori and Pasifika students. In P. Gluckman & H. Hayne (Eds.), *Improving the Transition: Reducing Social and Psychological Morbidity during Adolescence*. Auckland: Office of the Prime Minister's Science Advisory Committee.
5 Heckman (2011), p. 26.
6 Moynihan, D.P. (1965). *Employment, Income, and the Ordeal of the Negro Family*. Indianapolis: Bobbs-Merrill Company.
7 Coleman, J.S. (1966). *Equality of Educational Opportunity*. U.S. Washington, DC: Dept. of Health, Education, and Welfare, Office of Education.

8 Heckman (2011), p. 17.

9 May, S. (2009). *Pasifika Languages Strategy: Key Issues*. An unpublished briefing paper prepared for the Pasifika Languages Strategy. Wellington: Ministry of Pacific Island Affairs.

10 Bisin, A., & Verdier, T. (2000). Beyond the melting pot: Cultural transmission, marriage, and the evolution of ethnic and religious traits. *Quarterly Journal of Economics, 115*(3), 955–988. Fernandez, R., Fogli, A., & Olivetti, C. (2004). Mothers and sons: Preference formation and female labor force dynamics, *Quarterly Journal of Economics, 119*(4), 1249–1299; Grusec, Joan E., & Kuczynski, L. (1997). *Parenting and Children's Internalization of Values: A Handbook of Contemporary Theory*. New York: Wiley.

11 Polanyi, M. (1967). *The Tacit Dimension*. London: Routledge & Kegan Paul.

12 Archibugi, D., & Michie, J. (1995). Technology and innovation: An introduction. *Cambridge Journal of Economics, 19*(1), 1–4; Lundvall, B.A. (1992). *National Innovation System: Towards a Theory of Innovation and Interactive Learning*. Pinter, London.

13 Levinson, D.J. (1978). *The Seasons of a Man's Life*. New York: Random House Digital.

14 Earl, P.E. (1984). *The Corporate Imagination: How Big Companies Make Mistakes*. Wheatsheaf Books.

15 Olson, M. (1982). *The Rise and Decline of Nations*. New Haven: Yale University Press, p. 44.

16 Vaisey (2010).

17 Kao & Thompson (2003).

18 Lewis (1966).

19 Massey et al. (2014).

20 Heckman, J. (2011). The economics of inequality: The value of early childhood education. *American Educator, 35*(1), 31–47, p. 33.

21 Cobb-Clark, Salamanca, & Zhu (2016).

22 Harkness, S., Super, C.M., Axia, V., Eliasz, A., Palacios, J., & Welles-Nyström, B. (2001). Cultural pathways to successful parenting. *International Society for the Study of Behavior Development Newsletter, 38*, 9–11.

Index

For Product Safety Concerns and Information please contact our EU
representative GPSR@taylorandfrancis.com
Taylor & Francis Verlag GmbH, Kaufingerstraße 24, 80331 München, Germany

www.ingramcontent.com/pod-product-compliance
Ingram Content Group UK Ltd.
Pitfield, Milton Keynes, MK11 3LW, UK
UKHW022025061126
477531UK00002B/40
9780367616298